You're the
Umpire

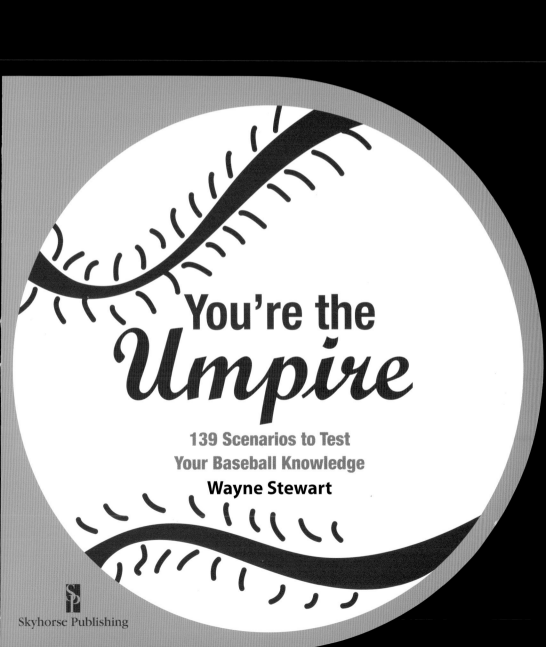

You're the
Umpire

139 Scenarios to Test
Your Baseball Knowledge

Wayne Stewart

Skyhorse Publishing

Skyhorse Publishing books may be purchased in bulk at special discounts for sales promotion, corporate gifts, fund raising, or educational purposes. Special editions can also be created to specifications. For details, contact Special Sales Department, Skyhorse Publishing, 555 Eighth Avenue, Suite 903, New York, NY 10018 or info@skyhorsepublishing.com.

www.skyhorsepublishing.com

10 9 8 7 6 5 4 3 2

Library of Congress Cataloging-in-Publication data is available on file.

ISBN: 978-1-60239-793-4

Printed in China

This book is dedicated to my wife of thirty-five plus years, Nancy, to our sons Scott and Sean, to our daughter-in-law Rachel, and to our grandson Nathan. Also to the memory of my father, O. J., who taught me to love words and their power, and my mother, Margaret, who taught me to love reading. Finally, this book is also respectfully dedicated to umpires everywhere.

CONTENTS

ALBERT PUJOLS

INTRODUCTION

Without question, umpiring is a demanding, difficult job. For many decades umpires didn't get a break during the season—they'd be lucky to spend any significant time at all with their families from spring training through September. Big league umps now work around 130 regular season games, getting four vacations of one week in length spread out over the season.

Once grossly underpaid, Major League Baseball's umpires today earn in the range of $100,000–$400,000 per season with most of them pulling down more than $200,000 as of 2008. In addition, they receive around $380 in per diem money and are provided with first-class tickets for their flights. By way of contrast, NBA referees gross between $90,000 and $225,000 for working a much shorter season (pro basketball has an eighty two-game regular season schedule while there are 162 games on baseball's schedule). Of course, umpires who work during the playoffs get extra compensation as well.

Imagine the scrutiny umpires are under, from their supervisors, from players, coaches, and managers, and from unforgiving fans. Major league umpire Fieldin Culbreth spoke of "the pressure of wanting to do well—this is the big leagues. It's played on TV; the whole world is watching." He estimated that he made between 200 and 300 calls every time he worked the plate, with about fifty of them being very close.

YOU'RE THE UMPIRE

Those fifty or so close calls place big league umps under a great deal of pressure, especially since the advent of the QuesTec system, which verifies home plate umpires' correct calls and coldly points out their mistakes on balls and strikes with digital precision. Culbreth believes umpires get calls correct about 99.7 percent of the time, yet Mike Port, Major League Baseball's vice president of umpiring, says about 55 percent of all games are still "observed firsthand" by Major League officials, with evaluation done on "missed calls, ejections, [and] other situations" beyond "the pitch-evaluation system." Umps, most of who put in around ten to twelve years in the minors, are also judged on "demeanor, hustle, form, [and] concentration."

"A good umpire is the umpire you don't even notice," said former American League president Ban Johnson. "He's there all afternoon but when the game is over, you don't remember his name." An umpire makes dozens of calls (hundreds if he's the man working behind the plate), yet if no player, coach, or manager got in his face, he quietly, unobtrusively did his job. Veteran umpire Tom Gorman agreed with Johnson's opinion, but added one corollary: "Once in a while a player will tell you that you worked a good game behind the plate, but when that happens it's always the winning pitcher who says it."

If an umpire does his job well over a long period of time, he *will* get noticed and earn respect from his peers, from the men who play and manage, and even, grudgingly, from fans. An umpire who is fair, makes the correct calls, and excels can even gain glory as a member of the Hall of Fame. Through 2009, just eight umpires were enshrined in Cooperstown, New York.

INTRODUCTION

Alex Grammas, who played for several big league clubs and coached (most notably on Cincinnati's "Big Red Machine" teams) and managed in the majors, said during a 2009 interview that Al Barlick (enshrined in 1989) was "the best ball and strike umpire [he ever saw]. He was a good umpire, period, but behind the plate he was as good as you'll ever see. I can't tell you [what made him better than the rest], but sometimes I watch games today on TV and they've got that little thing [computer-generated box on the screen] for the strike zone and balls will be four or five inches outside and they'll call it a strike. That's irritating. If they wanted that to be a strike, they'd have made the plate wider."

You're the Umpire was written to challenge baseball fans and also to help them better understand the rules of the game. Divided into three sections, the first, Routine Calls, presents scenarios that typically come up in games and involves clear-cut rules—fair and foul calls, strike zone questions, and the like. When possible, the situations come from actual games, but some scenarios submitted for your consideration, as Rod Serling used to say on *The Twilight Zone*, are made up to illustrate points or rules.

The next section, Basic Situations, deals with umpiring matters and rules that are just a bit more unusual or, for the casual fan, more obscure. Interference and obstruction calls, for example, don't occur too often, but they involve fairly standard rules that umps and knowledgeable fans know quite well.

In the final section, Obscure Rules and Situations, you will be presented with what baseball people call "knotty" problems. Here you will be asked questions involving the complex infield fly rule and other arcane matters. That section, then, will be the ultimate test of your umpiring skills and knowledge.

GOOD LUCK.

ROUTINE CALLS

It has often been said that the umpiring profession is a thankless job. Any call made on a "bang-bang" play is bound to tick off half of the players, coaches, and managers in the ballpark and perhaps close to 100 percent of the spectators when a call goes against the home team. But it is also an occupation fraught with hazard. After all, not too many jobs have spawned such a vengeful cry as "kill the umpire," and, in fact, umpires have, over the years, been showered with potentially lethal projectiles such as beer bottles fired by unruly, disgruntled fans. Johnny Evers, a Hall of Fame infielder of Tinker-to-Evers-to-Chance fame, went so far as to say that his "favorite umpire is a dead one." Umpire Al Forman once joked, "I occasionally get birthday cards from fans. But it's often the same message—they hope it's my last."

Umpires have even been attacked on the field of play. In 1940, George Magerkurth was wrestled to the ground and engaged in a fight with a spectator who had leapt over a railing and onto the field. It was later discovered that this fan was an ex-con who was not upset over a call, but had instead staged the scene to create a diversion. While all eyes were focused on the fracas, the convict had a pickpocket partner pilfering wallets and such from people in the stands. More recently, in April 2003, umpire Laz Diaz was accosted in the last half of the eighth inning by a drunken fan during a game between the Chicago White Sox and the Kansas City Royals.

DEREK JETER

A famous quote about the umpiring profession so widely referred to it's been variously attributed to Hall of Fame ump Nestor Chylak, Dick Stello, and Ed Runge (in slightly different forms) sums up the tribulation of umps. Basically, the line holds that fans "expect an umpire to be perfect on Opening Day and to improve as the season goes on."

An article in *Time* magazine once opined, "Ideally, the umpire should combine the integrity of a Supreme Court justice, the physical agility of an acrobat, the endurance of Job, and the imperturbability of Buddha." It's not easy.

The profession has been the source of many more interesting quotes. Leo "The Lip" Durocher once said, "I've never questioned the integrity of an umpire. Their eyesight, yes."

A famous story involves the Athletics' Jimmy Dykes doubting the eyesight of long-time umpire George Moriarty. Dykes had just been rung up on strikes and, highly displeased, he spun around on the ump. Then, surprisingly, instead of squawking, Dykes asked Moriarty how he spelled his name. The story has it Moriarty was puzzled but complied. Dykes then unloaded his punch line: "Just as I thought, only one *i*."

Umpire Bruce Froemming worked for a record thirty-seven big league seasons, was behind the dish for eleven no-hitters, and is one of only two umpires to work in over five thousand big league contests. He left no doubt that his eyesight was beyond question when he stated, "I can see the sun okay and that's 93,000,000 miles away."

Then there was Cal Hubbard, who once admonished hitters, "Boys, I'm one of those umpires that misses 'em every once in a while, so if it's close, you'd better hit it."

The legendary Bill Klem, another Hall of Fame umpire, famously quipped, "It ain't nothin' till I call it." Once, after being shown a picture of a play from the previous day—a photo that revealed he had missed the call—he retorted, "Gentlemen, he was out because I said he was out." Klem also got the last word in when slugger Hack Wilson angrily accused Klem of having missed a pitch. The unflappable Klem retorted, "Maybe, but I wouldn't have if I had a bat."

There is no doubt an umpire has to take command and to exude confidence, to sell his calls and to take some guff, but not *too* much. Larry Goetz, a National League umpire for twenty-two seasons, said, "It isn't enough for an umpire to merely know what he's doing. He has to *look* as though he knows what's he's doing, too."

Brett Locher, an umpire with more than thirty years of experience at the amateur level, learned an important lesson when he had the opportunity to speak with big league ump Ron Luciano. The colorful Luciano told him that "even if you're not sure of the call, make sure you always sell it." Later, on a close call at first base that Locher conceded he "couldn't tell whether the guy was safe or out," he called the runner out and went over the top doing so. "Not one person said anything," Locher recalled. Everyone must have figured, as legendary broadcaster Bob Prince used to say, "They got him out by a gnat's eyelash."

Normally, the last thing an umpire wants to do is what minor league umpire Ralph DeLeonardis once did. After missing a call, he explained with a liberal dose of self-deprecating humor, "Well, I blew it the way I saw it." Of course, when long-time National League umpire Augie Donatelli was asked if he had ever blown a call, he flashed a grin and his wit, replying, "Do you think I'd admit it?"

When an umpire makes the correct call, he gets little, if any, credit. As thirty-year veteran Major League umpire Doug Harvey lamented, "When I am right, no one remembers. When I am wrong, no one forgets." (Perhaps that's why Harvey seemed resentful of players in general, saying, "They're all a bunch of crybabies, especially the small-change hitters.") Chylak would concur with Harvey about umpires not being appreciated. He felt umpiring was the "only job in America that everybody knows how to do better than the guy who's doing it."

Tom Gorman, a National League umpire for twenty-five seasons, didn't think *all* baseball players were whiners. "The bigger the guy, the less he argues," Gorman said. "You never heard a word out of Stan Musial or Willie Mays or Roberto Clemente. They never tried to make you look bad." Gorman was also the umpire who said, hopefully only facetiously, "Anytime I got those bang-bang plays at first base, I called them out. It made the game shorter."

Yet another humorous take on the job came from Dusty Boggess, a National League umpire from 1944 to 1962. He had just rung up Chicago Cubs catcher Clyde McCullough on strikes and the player disputed the third strike. Boggess replied, "You know, Mac, for twenty years as a player I thought that was a ball, too; but it's a strike, so I went to umpiring."

Finally, there were the words of Tim Hurst, an umpire at the turn of the twentieth century with an optimistic view of his occupation: "The pay is good, it keeps you out in the fresh air and sunshine, and you can't beat the hours."

YOU'RE THE UMPIRE

All of these quotes reveal various facets of umpires and their attitudes, but now it's time for you to don the gear and uniform of an ump and become a member of a group that was once known as "the men in blue." Major League Baseball employs sixty-eight umpires, enough to cover the maximum number of venues that could host games on a given night (fifteen) and spell the two crews who are on vacation each week. You now, in effect, become the sixty-ninth umpire.

In this section of the book you will be tested on your knowledge of routine plays, such as what determines whether a batted ball is fair or foul. Picture the scenarios in your mind and boldly make your calls.

○ ○ ○

(1) Let's say Albert Pujols of the St. Louis Cardinals is up to bat. This slugger normally hits with sufficient force to set seismograph needles violently twitching. In this plate appearance he gets an inside pitch from Roy Oswalt of the Houston Astros. Pujols's quick hands lash out and he sends a hot smash down the third base line. The ball takes one hop in fair territory, slashes directly over the third base bag, strikes the ground in foul territory, and jets its way into the left field corner. Carlos Lee retrieves the ball and gets it into his cutoff man but not before Pujols steams into second base. What's your call—is it a double for the Cardinal superstar or do you call it a foul ball and send him back to the batter's box?

Answer on page **35**

ROUTINE CALLS

(2) Imagine Boston Red Sox designated hitter David Ortiz lifts a deep fly ball down the right field line on an 0-and-1 count. Jacoby Ellsbury, who had tripled, goes back to the bag to tag up. New York Yankees right fielder Nick Swisher gives chase and finally catches up to the ball. He had one foot inside the foul line and one in foul grounds as he first made contact with the ball, which, if untouched, would have landed in foul territory. The ball bounces in, then out, of his glove, falling to the ground. Ellsbury took off for home the moment Swisher put leather on the ball and scored easily. What ruling would a big league ump make here?

Answer on pages **35–36**

(3) Here's the simplest fair-versus-foul ruling that you'll ever encounter (simple, but sometimes requiring great eyesight on the part of umpires). A line drive off the bat of San Francisco Giants superstar Willie Mays screams by third baseman Eddie Mathews of the old Milwaukee Braves and lands on the left field line, kicking up a bit of chalk. Is this a fair ball or a foul ball?

Answer on page **36**

(4) Baseball announcers often mention the fact that various umpires seem to have their own strike zones (more so years ago than nowa-days). That is to say some umps, for example, tend to call low pitches strikes while taking away higher pitches, calling them balls, while

other umpires do just the opposite. Some are very generous and have a wide strike zone; some have a very narrow strike zone. For that matter, sometimes a given umpire (though not too often now in the majors) may start a game seemingly calling pitches one way, say, giving the pitchers a lot of leeway, then, suddenly, tighten things up, prompting pitchers, catchers, and managers to gripe. "You're squeezing my pitcher," a manager or catcher snarls. After all, most baseball people say they have few complaints about a home plate umpire's toil as long as he is consistent.

However, it certainly seems to the average baseball fan that it is not okay for an umpire to have his *own* strike zone; his job is simply to enforce *the* strike zone. First of all, what if a batter is an excellent low-ball hitter (Stan Musial once joked that he was a low-ball hitter and a highball drinker) playing in a game in which the opposing pitcher made his living on high pitches (admittedly not a likely scenario), with many of his offerings coming just out of the rule book's strike zone? Or, what if the pitcher had great control and knew the plate ump would give him the high strike? In either event the poor batter is handcuffed as he will see no low offerings to his liking and will have to chase after high stuff or be penalized by a called strike if he doesn't swing at those pitches.

The trend in the latter part of the twentieth century was toward small strike zones, helping to fuel the already beefed up offenses in the game and leading to pitchers angrily chirping that the strike zone had become about the same size as a copy of the *Sporting News*. Reliever Jesse Orosco, who pitched from 1979 to 2003, appearing in more games at the time of his retirement (1,252) than any pitcher ever, saw a "Honey I Shrunk the Strike Zone" trend as he neared the end of his career. Although he wasn't elated by the turn of events, he philosophized, "Umpires have their set ways. I'm sure they're doing the best job they can. I know I've thrown pitches where I thought they were strikes, but I know if I go out there and start arguing I'm going to get away from my game. So I've got to respect what an umpire is doing."

He added, "All umpires are different—some have a low strike zone, some are high. I watch games for the first few innings on TV [at the ballpark] to see what the strike zone looks like so I know what it'll be like during the game. So when I go out there I'm prepared."

Alex Grammas grumbled that too often pitches off the plate are called strikes. "You see these analysts on television who are ex-pitchers say, 'Yeah, that was close enough,' but if you're a hitter, you don't think so."

It may also irritate fans that superstars get the benefit of calls, especially close ones, but that remains a fact of baseball life. He may have been exaggerating somewhat, but Ron Luciano once stated, "If Rod Carew has two strikes on him and fouls off five pitches and then takes the sixth down the middle, I'm calling it a ball."

Ideally, the bottom line is this: An umpire's job is, across the board, to enforce the rules. In theory at least, all players should get the same fair shake and a player shouldn't have to adapt to an umpire; the strike zone shouldn't contract or expand according to the whim or personal interpretation of umpires from night to night.

To be fair, the ump's side of the story is this: Thanks to QuesTec and to a change in the delineation of the zone, and because the two league's umpiring staffs joined into one unit, the strike zone, said umpire Dale Scott, is now "called more consistently and was written than ever before." He also noted the zone is stated clearly in the rule book, "but is up to the umpire's judgment."

Veteran big league umpire Fieldin Culbreth added, "I can assure you that when [an umpire] says he's calling his strike zone, what he's referring to is he's the one that's umpiring the strike zone that day—that's the reason it's *his* strike zone. Every single person that ever comes behind that plate is doing his absolute best to conform to the strike zone that is written in that rule book. However, and this is my interpretation of it, there are no strings out there in front of home plate that happen to magically light up when a ball either goes inside of it or goes outside of it. There's this imaginary box out there suspended over this thing that's lying down on the ground, and I'm having to tell you where I think those definitions are."

He compared umpires to players, but said that while one player might hit .350 and another only .180, "all of them make up a team and all of them are vital to making up the team." However, with players, "the guy who hits .350, for some reason he has just honed his skills better than the guy that hits .180," but the disparity between the prowess of various umpires when calling balls and strikes is nowhere near that wide. "Some people might see that pitch just a hair low and that's just because that's the way he sees it. So when they refer to it as 'my strike zone,' it truly is your strike zone because there might be slight—and when I mean slight, I mean *very* slight—variations between what is and what isn't a strike from umpire to umpire to umpire.

"And the reason I know this to be true is because with the invent of QuesTec and the ZE [Zone Evaluation] system that they have now in all the ballparks that tracks the pitches that we're somewhat evaluated from, I can tell you that as a staff we're talking about a pitch or two per game that separates the top from the bottom. So it's obvious we can still use the words 'my strike zone,' but that doesn't mean I'm making up a totally different one [from other umps when they work the plate]."

All of this (finally) leads to your question: Just what are the parameters of the strike zone nowadays? Naturally, to be a called strike the ball must pass over the area above home plate, a target that is seventeen inches wide (and, yes, even if a slight portion of the ball nips any of the black perimeter of the plate, a pitch is a strike), but what are the highest and lowest points, in relationship to each batter, for strikes?

Answer on pages **36–37**

15

YOU'RE THE UMPIRE

5 One of the most blatant cases of an umpire giving a pitcher a wide strike zone took place when the Atlanta Braves faced the Florida Marlins in Miami in the pivotal Game Five of the National League Championship Series on October 12, 1997. The Braves starting pitcher worked seven innings and chalked up nine strikeouts versus one walk surrendered and reliever Mike Cather added another strikeout. Meanwhile, Florida's rookie hurler seemed to get every close call, painting the very broad corners and racking up fifteen strikeouts (against just one walk issued). That total was good enough to establish a new record for NLCS play, and it remains one of the highest strikeout totals in post-season history.

Your job here is to name any one of the three principal players in that historic day's drama—the home plate ump, the Atlanta starter, or the Florida starting pitcher.

Answer on pages **37–40**

6 One tremendous sight to behold is baseball's most beautiful ballet: the crisply executed, acrobatic double play. However, not all twin killings are so eye pleasing; some aren't even "clean."

Let's imagine Cleveland Indians star center fielder Grady Sizemore singles to lead off a game. The next batter, shortstop Asdrubal Cabrera, sends a slow roller to Boston Red Sox shortstop Nick Green, who fires the ball to second baseman Dustin Pedroia, who is coming across the bag at second base. Pedroia receives the ball a split second *after* he has cut across second, taking a quick step into the infield grass to avoid the sliding Sizemore, who is quickly and violently barreling down on him to break up the possible double play. Pedroia then fires the ball to Kevin Youkilis at first to nip Cabrera. What's the call by the second base ump; is this a twin killing?

Answer on pages **40–41**

(7) Another fair-or-foul question. Chad Tracy of the Arizona Diamondbacks is fooled by a pitch from Chicago's Ted Lilly and fouls it off. The ball hits behind the plate then rolls into fair territory where Lilly pounces on it and lobs it to Cubs first baseman Derrek Lee. Is this a foul ball or an out?

Answer on page **41**

(8) What would happen if a batter hit a ball straight down, which first struck the ground inside the batter's box, then bounced up and popped the hitter on his chin before rolling weakly out toward the mound? Can the pitcher make a play on the ball? Is the ball dead once it hit the batter?

Answer on page **41**

(9) Let's say the same batter tried to drag a bunt. The ball took one hop in fair territory and hit the batter, who is part way out of the box, with one foot planted on the ground as he is making his way to first. The ball, we'll say, touched him while it was in fair territory.

Answer on page **42**

(10) The Cincinnati Reds have loaded the bases, and have only spent one out doing so. Now Barry Larkin is at bat and he taps the ball in such a way it trickles just inches into fair territory. The opposing catcher, Mike Piazza of the New York Mets, secures the ball at the same time he accidentally has one foot on the plate. Pivoting a bit, he hurls the ball toward first but his peg is errant and flies into right field, enabling all of the runners, including the batter, to advance two bases. What's the ruling on this play which, really if you think it through, is quite basic?

Answer on page **42**

(11) Hanley Ramirez is on third base with two men out and, in this imaginary play, he bolts from his walking lead as the pitcher begins a slow windup. Let's say he actually slides across the plate just a microsecond after Dan Uggla hits a sharp grounder to the shortstop, who throws to first to retire the sides. Does the run count as Ramirez scored prior to the out being recorded at first?

Answer on page **42**

(12) Similar scenario: One man is aboard and two men are out. We'll stick with Ramirez as the runner, having just doubled off the fence. Then

Jorge Cantu rips a ball toward the gap in right-center and feels he can (and should try to with two down) get himself into scoring position. Ramirez crosses home, just as in the previous question, with a fraction of a second to spare before Cantu is gunned out trying to stretch his single into a double. Does this make matters different than the previous question or not?

Answer on page **42**

(13) Let's imagine Albert Belle is unhappy (and with his infamous fiery temper this one's not much of a stretch of the imagination) about the home plate umpire's strike zone on two of the first pitches he sees. Moments later, he is rung up on a borderline call which sets off the powder keg and Belle goes ballistic, unleashing a string of invectives audible twenty rows into the seats behind the plate. Where does an umpire draw the line—normally, what does it take to get a player ejected?

Answer on pages **42–46**

(14) In 1991, the Minnesota Twins matched up against the Atlanta Braves in the World Series. Both teams had completed a rare worst-to-first comeback, having finished in the cellar of their division one year earlier.

An odd play took place in Game Two when Ron Gant of the Braves sent a line drive into the outfield for a solid single. He rounded the bag aggressively but realized he would have to scamper back to first when Twins left fielder Dan Gladden hustled the ball back into the infield. Gant made it back to first base standing up, well ahead of a throw to first sacker Kent Hrbek. That didn't stop Hrbek from applying a forceful sweep tag on Gant, a tag so strong Gant's foot came off the bag. Is Gant safe or out?

Answer on page **46**

(15) Say speedy Sonny Jackson of the Braves, circa 1969, hits a tapper to Cubs third baseman Ron Santo, who makes a strong peg to Ernie Banks at first. The ball and the runner arrive at first base at the same time. What does an umpire do in such a situation?

Answer on page **47**

(16) In this next scenario, Ty Cobb hits a ball hard, it bounces off home plate then becomes a very high Baltimore chop. Cobb easily beats out the throw to first. However, if the ball struck home plate first, isn't this merely a foul ball?

Answer on page **47**

(17) Easy one: The Toronto Blue Jays have the bases loaded but two men are out. Vernon Wells whiffs but Yankees catcher Jorge Posada can't hold on to the ball. By the time he retrieves it he decides it's safer to stomp on home plate for the side-retiring out rather than risk a throw to first to retire the batter. Is this tactic permissible?

Answer on page **47**

(18) On August 6, 2004, in the last half of the tenth inning of a 1–1 contest, speedy Carl Crawford was the runner off third in a bases loaded situation for Tampa Bay. Tino Martinez lifted a fly ball to left field, apparently deep enough to score Crawford, who then edged back toward third base to tag up. Meanwhile, the Mariners' shortstop, Jose Lopez, believing he had nothing to lose, intentionally placed himself where he would screen Crawford's view of Raul Ibanez's imminent catch. If Crawford's tagging up from third was delayed a second or so by his impaired vision, Lopez calculated, perhaps he would either hold up or be shot down at the plate. Is this ploy a legal one?

Answer on page **47**

(19) A batter—let's say it's all-time great Cap Anson—has a 2–2 count on him when he decides to fool the defense, which is playing back, surprising them with a bunt. The pitch is a bit high and instead of laying it down, he fouls it off. What's the call in this situation?

Answer on pages **47–48**

(20) Hall of Fame umpire Jocko Conlan—known to be as tough as not merely nails, but rusty railroad spikes—once related the time slow-footed Bobby Bragan of the Brooklyn Dodgers was on first when the speedy Pete Reiser came to the plate in a game in which they trailed the Cubs 2–1. With two men retired, Reiser crushed a gap shot and tried to stretch a sure double into a triple. He was thrown out, however,

on a close play. Meanwhile, Bragan had not yet scored. Still chugging, he finally touched home plate. Does his run count?

Answer on page **48**

(21) Joe Sewell struck out just 114 times in the course of 7,132 big league at bats. He also was involved in an unusual play as a third baseman for the Yankees. Chicago White Sox hitter Lew Fonseca laid a bunt down the line which Sewell soon realized he could get to, but not before Fonseca would have a guaranteed single. Pitcher Red Ruffing also charged over to the ball, but Sewell shouted, "Let it roll." At that moment, recalled Sewell, he used his spikes to carve "a trench across the foul line at a 45-degree angle." The ball, like the course of a river diverted by a dam, changed its path and rolled foul. What's the proper call here?

Answer on page **48**

(22) Bobby Bragan recalled managing a game in the Pacific Coast League in which "the umpire blew a couple of calls. I went out to protest. I said, 'You know you're making a joke of the game. I'm going to show you how to make a joke out of it.' I sent nine pinch hitters up for the batter. I told them, 'Don't let him pitch; just let them announce you as a hitter and I'll call you out and send somebody else up.' Right before a pitch, I'd call [each pinch hitter] back." Is this legal?

Answer on page **48**

(23) Another story and scenario from the colorful Bragan. When he was with the Pittsburgh Pirates, he managed identical twins Johnny and Eddie O'Brien. "In spring training," confessed Bragan many years later, "if it got to, say, the seventh inning and I needed a hitter, I would have John go in and put Eddie's uniform on, have him go out and pinch hit, tell [the umpire], 'Eddie O'Brien batting for the pitcher.'" Given the informality of spring training, is this move permissible?

Answer on pages **48–49**

(24) From cardinals to orioles, baseball and birds go together, and in more ways than nicknames. Randy Johnson, "The Big Unit," once hit a bird in mid-flight with a fastball, pulverizing the poor animal. A Dave Winfield warm-up throw on August 4, 1983, struck and killed a seagull in Toronto. Fans showered him with catcalls and various objects. In fact, after the contest he was taken to an Ontario police station where he was charged with cruelty to animals even though Winfield contended he did not intentionally hit the bird. All charges were dropped the next day.

Now, on June 11, 2009, at Cleveland's Progressive Field, with Mark DeRosa on second base in the last half of the tenth inning, representing the potential winning run, Indians' hitter Shin-Soo Choo slapped a sinking line drive against pitcher Kyle Farnsworth of the Kansas City Royals. The ball skipped off the grass in shallow center field and then struck the wing of a seagull which had just begun to take flight after it had been, just moments earlier, walking around near Royals center fielder Coco Crisp. In fact, the ball changed its path after hitting the seagull, skipped away from Crisp, and rolled on to the outfield wall.

The outfielder was livid over the odd occurrence, believing he might have otherwise had a play at the plate. The gull, stunned momentarily, eventually flew away rather groggily, minus one feather, but what about Choo and DeRosa? DeRosa apparently scored the winning run, but would you freeze him at third and call a dead ball here? Is this a judgment call—if the umpires felt Crisp was right that he did have a play on DeRosa, could they declare him out due to interference?

Answer on page **49**

(25) Cubs outfielder Milton Bradley, a veritable magnet for controversy throughout his career, had a rough day on defense on June 12, 2009. It began when the right fielder lost a pop fly off the bat of Minnesota's Jason Kubel in the seventh inning of an interleague game. Shortly after that, he got a poor jump on a fly ball hit by Michael Cuddyer, allowing a key run to cross home. It was the Twins' fifth run in a game they would go on to win 7–4.

Then, just one inning later, Minnesota had Nick Punto on third and Brendan Harris on first with one man down. Joe Mauer hit a fly ball, predictably—almost as if scripted—to Bradley, who hauled it in then, believing he had caught the inning's third out, posed for several seconds before throwing the baseball into the seats. Punto tagged up and scored on what was recorded as a sacrifice fly, but what of Harris—where do you place him?

Answer on pages **49–50**

(26) It could happen only in New York City and only with the ineptitude of the '62 Mets. New York's colorful first baseman "Marvelous" Marv Throneberry was involved in what Solly Hemus said was the funniest play he ever saw. It took place on June 17 during the Mets' inaugural season, the year the hapless expansion club went on to lose a record 120 games, winning exactly one quarter of their decisions. (The premodern day record for games dropped was 134 defeats suffered by the Cleveland Spiders in 1899, translating to a miserable win-loss percentage of just .134—the lowest ever in big league baseball.)

Hemus, a Mets coach in 1962 and 1963, narrated, "We were playing [the Cubs] and were behind by one run and had two men on base [Gene Woodling on second and Frank Thomas on first]. He hits a 'triple' in right-center. What happened is when Throneberry rounded first, he missed the bag. When he slid into third base, the umpire there called him safe. A player picked up the ball and threw to *second*. They called him out [on the appeal]."

Mets manager Casey Stengel ran out onto the field and argued the play. He wanted to check that the umpires were positive that they clearly saw his runner miss the bag and he wanted to be sure the runs that scored on the hit counted. Do any of the runners actually score?

Answer on pages **50–51**

(27) Easy one: On April 18, 1954, Chicago Cubs hurler Paul Minner had retired nineteen straight after giving up a single to the game's leadoff hitter. Six innings later, with one man out, Chicago held a 3–0 lead when Wally Moon rapped a single to center. Red Schoendienst followed by making an out which brought Cardinal superstar Stan Musial up to bat. He scorched a double to the right field corner to drive Moon home. When Cubs third baseman Randy Jackson mishandled the relay throw and then made a wild peg, Musial scored.

Things looked good for St. Louis until first base umpire Lee Ballanfant finally was able to notify both teams that he had called Musial's poke foul. Was there anything the Cardinals could do about the situation?

Answer on page **52**

(28) Let's say Andruw Jones is at the plate and gets a 3–0 fastball right down the pipe. He rips the ball savagely, drilling a line drive through the box, but his sweeping backswing hits catcher Ivan Rodriguez in his head gear. What bearing on the play does this contact have? Is the ball dead, does he lose his single, or is the ball in play?

Answer on page **52**

ROUTINE CALLS

(29) There is one out in the top of the first inning and nobody on base when, with the count 2–2 on Houston's Lance Berkman, he swings and misses. The catcher, Atlanta's Brian McCann, fails to catch the ball cleanly and it trickles off his glove and bounds a few yards off to his right. Berkman decides to light off for first base. Is this permitted? Isn't he retired on the strikeout?

Answer on page **52**

(30) Same scenario only this time a fellow Astro is on first base prior to Berkman's strikeout. What difference does that factor make on this play?

Answer on page **52**

(31) One more time: On this occasion everything is the same as the previous situation except now there are two men out before Berkman fans. How does that difference impact this play?

Answer on pages **52–53**

(32) What can you do to punish a manger that has already been kicked out of a game yet continues to behave badly? In June 2009, Baltimore skipper Dave Trembley was ejected from the game in the first inning of the O's game against the Mariners for arguing a base-running call. In theory, managers who are booted from games are not to take part in the game in any way, but they often do—frequently communicating their strategic moves clandestinely to coaches who then carry out their manager's wishes.

In this case, though, Trembley got caught. He later told the media that one of his players, Luke Scott, had come into the club-house during the game and Trembley asked him to "get me a couple" runs. What can an umpire do in this situation?

Answer on page **53**

(33) Let's say Todd Helton was batting and a pitch from Cliff Lee bounced in front of the plate and then somehow got lodged in his catcher's face mask. If nobody was on base, it's no big deal, but what if a runner was leading off second base? Would you call dead ball with no advance by the runner or would you allow the runner to take third base?

Answer on page **53**

(34) The Red Sox decide to issue an intentional walk to Yankee slugger Alex Rodriguez. Pitcher Tim Wakefield aims the ball well out of the strike zone toward his catcher Jason Varitek, who is standing fully upright, ready to skip a step or two outside of his position in the catcher's box. Just as the ball leaves Wakefield's hand Varitek vacates the box. Is this or isn't this a case of a catcher's balk?

Answer on page **53**

(35) Say Seattle's perennial Gold Glove winner Ichiro Suzuki goes after a ball that is tailing away from him toward foul territory. He has the ball

in his glove for a split second and then makes contact with either another player or, say, the railing of the stands, causing the ball to jar loose and hit the ground in foul territory. Is it an out or merely a foul ball?

Answer on page **53**

(36) This one should be a routine call for you if you think it through. The St. Louis Cardinals traveled to Philadelphia on July 24, 2009, and, in the bottom half of the fifth inning Pedro Feliz hit a ground ball to Cards shortstop Brendan Ryan. Ryan scooped the ball up just inches away from the cut of the grass where the infield meets the outfield and made a long throw to Albert Pujols at first. The ball pulled Pujols off the bag, forcing him to leap high for the catch. Then, as he came down, he did so directly on the bag resulting in a photo finish between his right foot and the right foot of Feliz. In fact, and here's the key to this question, Feliz's foot landed on top of Pujols's. What's the call here—is Feliz safe or out?

Answer on page **53**

(37) Here's another easy one if you play detective and pay attention to all the clues/data concerning an unusual bunt. On July 20, 2009, an odd play took place when Rafael Furcal of the Los Angeles Dodgers faced Cincinnati pitcher Micah Owings. Furcal, a deer-swift runner, bunted the ball over the head of third baseman Edwin Encarnacion, who

had begun to charge in when he first saw Furcal show bunt. The ball landed on the infield dirt, nearly at the point where the dirt meets the outfield grass, then spun into foul territory in the vicinity of shallow left field, allowing Furcal to hustle into second base.

At first it appeared that Furcal, a switch hitter batting lefty against Owings, was attempting a drag bunt toward first base, but he angled his bat and took a rather hard chop at the ball as he ran up on the pitch. Now, we know his bunt is legal, so the only question is, from the info provided, is the ball fair or foul?

Answer on page **54**

(38) Cleveland's Luis Valbuena was in the batter's box on July 28, 2009, facing Matt Palmer of the Angels. Valbuena called time out, stepped out of the box, and then, fearing that Palmer was about to throw the ball anyway, hopped right back into the box. Why didn't he just remain outside of the box? After all, he had called time out.

Answer on page **54**

(39) Say Ernie Banks is at the plate and he hits a ball which takes a quick hop near his feet while he's still in the box. The ball then ricochets and hits Banks on one of his shins. What's the call here?

Answer on page **54**

(40) This time a batter, let's imagine Mickey Mantle, decides to bunt—picture Mantle dragging the ball in an effort to beat out the bunt,

ready to ramble down the line with his blazing speed—but the ball bounces and hits him while he's on his way to first, in fair ground and clearly no longer in the batter's box. Does this factor change things from the previous question? What's your call?

Answer on pages **54–55**

(41) This odd one took place on July 18, 2009. With the Los Angeles Dodgers up 3–0 and men on first and second with two out in the sixth, Houston's Mike Hampton gave up a line drive single to left by Mark Loretta allowing Casey Blake to score from second and Matt Kemp to scoot around to third on the play at the plate. When catcher Humberto Quintero couldn't apply the tag to the sliding Blake, he handed the ball over to Hampton, who was backing up the play.

A frustrated Hampton fired the ball toward his glove, but, remarkably, missed and the ball grazed off the thumb of his glove, sailing into foul territory near the stands. By the time he retrieved the ball Kemp had stepped on home plate and Loretta had moved up a base as well. What ruling should you make on Hampton's gaff?

Answer on page **55**

(42) On a few occasions something so bizarre happens on a baseball field umpires have to call upon a rarely used rule. For example, in Cleveland the team ran a promotion known as Ten-Cent Beer Night on June 4, 1974. It was an ill-advised and nightmarish promo as many

of the 25,135 fans on hand guzzled gallons of beer at a mere dime a pop, became inebriated, and stormed onto the diamond. At the time of the stampede the Indians were tied with the Rangers with two out and the bases jammed in the last half of the ninth.

"I was pitching on the Ten-Cent Beer Night," recalled Texas hurler Steve Foucault. "People were throwing chairs on the field and I got hit in the face with a cup in the eye and Jeff Burroughs got hit with something. There were about three of us that went to the hospital [as a precaution]."

Another time, on July 12, 1979, the Chicago White Sox, under the management of the colorful Veecks, Bill and son Mike, held Disco Demolition Night. A throng of over 50,000 packed the park, awaiting the anti-disco festivities to be held between games of a double-header. Those who brought a disco record to Comiskey Park were charged only 98 cents to spin the turnstiles and enter the twinbill.

Things soon took an ugly turn. Rowdy fans "Frisbeed" a ton of vinyl records onto the field during the first contest. After the game a local disc jockey blew up a pile of disco records and records left over were ignited, creating a bonfire. It was then that about 5,000 spectators rushed onto the field turning it into a shambles. When fans refused to clear the diamond, riot police eventually drove the mob back into the stands, but it was too late—the field was unplayable.

ROUTINE CALLS

In both cases, once the fans became totally unruly and out of control, the umpires were forced to take a drastic action. What should umpires do in the midst of such bedlam?

Answer on pages 55–57

(43) Looking back over his long career, Bruce Froemming recalled, "The biggest play I had was in Houston, Texas, my first year. It was a play at second base with the Phillies and the Astros. The Phillies had the bags loaded, they're down, 4–3, with one out, and Deron Johnson hit a shot to second base and the second baseman flipped the ball to [Houston shortstop] Roger Metzger coming across the bag and Tim McCarver hit him with a football block. He was way outside the three-foot area … and, meanwhile, they had scored two runs on the play because the ball was laying in center field." What was Froemming's ruling?

Answer on page 57

HANLEY RAMIREZ

ANSWERS

(1) It's a fair ball. The position of the ball as it travels by or over the bag is the key here. Homer "Duke" Rash, a former minor league umpire, stated, "A lot of people think that because it hit in foul territory, that it's foul, but it's not because it went over some part of the bag—even if it's the outside edge of the bag. It's still a fair ball." Pujols gets his double.

Similarly, if a batted ball hits a base, it's fair no matter what path it takes after striking that base.

By the way, Rash recalled that when he first signed a pro contract in an era in which Class D umpires earned about $250 to $375 per month, "They [the league officials] didn't want me using my first name Homer because a homer refers to an umpire whose calls favor the home team." So they agreed on his old nickname, "Duke."

(2) This is a foul ball, nothing but a deeply hit strike, in effect, for Ortiz; send Ellsbury back to third.

The factor which determines whether the ball should be called fair or foul here is the location of the ball, not the fielder. Thus, even if a fielder who is "in bounds" (regardless of whether he has one or both feet in fair territory) makes contact with the ball, the ball must be called foul if its path was such that it would have landed in foul territory had it not been touched. Likewise, if a fielder standing in foul grounds reached back into fair territory and touched a ball that was destined to hit inside the foul line, it's a fair ball—once more, forget about where he is positioned, and consider only the ball and the foul line. It would even be a fair ball if, say, by touching the ball that was destined to fall into play in fair grounds he deflected it into foul territory.

In a somewhat related matter, if an outfielder has the opportunity to catch a foul ball but knew that by doing so a runner off third base would score, for example, a vital or winning run, he may, of course, not touch the ball at all, thus preventing the runner from tagging up.

(3) Any ball hitting the foul line or, for that matter, the foul pole, is a fair ball—likewise, if a nubber down the first or third base line came to rest while touching any part of the chalk of the foul line, it's a fair ball. Some consider the name foul pole a misnomer, that it should be called the fair pole—in fact there is a book on baffling baseball issues entitled *Why Is the Foul Pole Fair?*—but one imagines that basically the name was given to this boundary simply because it separates fair territory from foul ground and marks where that region begins.

(4) In order for a pitch to be called a strike, it must be no higher than the point midway between the top of the hitter's shoulders and the top of his uniform pants (roughly around the bottom of his rib cage) and

no lower than the hollow below his kneecap. Of course, the batter may not alter his stance to shrink his strike zone as umpires are supposed to define each hitter's zone as his normal, natural stance as he is ready to swing at a pitch.

(5) The umpire was Eric Gregg, the Braves pitcher was Greg Maddux, and the record-tying pitcher for the Marlins was Livan Hernandez. The day before Hernandez's gem, Mike Mussina of the Baltimore Orioles had also chalked up fifteen Ks, although in a losing cause.

Hernandez, a twenty-two-year-old rookie who won his game 2–1, just two days after he had pitched out of the bullpen, must have been thinking, "Gee, there's nothing to pitching up here in the bigs," after firing his masterful three-hit complete game. Actually, on the regular season he had not gone the distance once.

One report claimed Gregg extended his strike zone by roughly twelve inches on both sides of the plate, and, around this time period, the media had begun getting upset with umpires' growing trend to widen the zone. They also felt Gregg's definition of the strike zone and his ball-strike calls had, as author Bruce Weber put it, "indisputably altered the quality of the game." In fact, the Braves' final batter, Fred McGriff, was called out looking on a pitch some said was a foot or more outside. He and some teammates, realizing the breadth of the strike zone that day, had to flail at such pitches much of the day. It was little wonder Atlanta managed only three hits.

After the game Gregg said of his performance, "If you know me, you know my strike zone." Once again, such comments irk fans who feel umpires should stick to enforcing the rule book precepts and not create their own. Sure, there is the element of humans making mistakes and being individuals—umps aren't robots, they will vary a bit from man to man—but the strike zone should not belong, per se, to a given ump and Gregg did take flak for his calls that day.

Fieldin Culbreth said that nowadays strike zones are much more consistent across the board. "I can tell you that in 2009, my strike zone and Gary Cederstrom's strike zone, and Brian O'Nora's, and whoever's—I will guarantee you they're just about as uniform as they can be.

"Our strike zones are looked at every single night. Again, it's just another one of those perceptions or misconceptions that people think just because somebody says 'my strike zone' or 'this guy's got [his own zone].' I can tell you that's just not the truth any more; that's not the way it is."

Incidentally, the all-time record for the most batters fanned in a postseason game belongs to Bob Gibson, who set seventeen Detroit Tigers down in the Game One of the 1968 World Series.

Hall of Famer Ozzie Smith once commented, "I think umpires have too much power . . . the more money a player makes, the more the umpire tries to show off that power to him. Unfortunately, since I signed my [large] contract my strike zone has suddenly become a lot larger."

ROUTINE CALLS

Over the years it has not been unusual for established star pitchers, men who are always around the plate and can hit their spots such as Maddux, to get strikes called on pitches a half a foot off the plate. When the Devil Rays hosted Atlanta on July 2, 1998, a dandy of a pitchers' match-up took place. The Braves' starter was Maddux, the perennial Cy Young winner, who entered the game with an 11–2 ledger. Tampa Bay threw rookie sensation Rolando Arrojo, then 10–4 on the year and bound for the All-Star Game.

After the contest, a win for Maddux, a defeat for Arrojo, Devil Rays shortstop Kevin Stocker said the game had not just been a match-up of two torrid pitchers, "It's not that simple. It's Maddux *and* the umpire against Arrojo and the umpire." In other words, the home plate umpire called the game as if he were two different people (or one man with two different strike zones), depending upon which pitcher was on the mound. "Maddux gets another four inches off the plate," Stocker said. "It was tough to see Rolando not get calls. You have to realize, this is Maddux; Rolando is a rookie." He felt it was a case of a double standard being involved in the outcome of the game.

Former pitcher Jim Brosnan once said Warren Spahn didn't throw a pitch "over the middle fourteen inches of the plate the last couple years he played, unless it was 3–0 and the batter was taking. . . . The umpires have to know you can do certain things, realize that you're trying to do them, and then they start giving you pitches."

Umpire Marty Springstead told Bruce Weber that if an ump squeezed the strike zone too much, the game will go too slowly with batters taking pitch after pitch. While he stated an umpire can't help a pitcher who is way too wild by stretching the strike zone as if it were made of elastic, he could and would call strikes which he knew were a few inches off the plate, meaning his strike zone could be as wide as nineteen inches (the width of the plate inches plus two more inches of leeway). "Now, if you can't hit a pitch that's nineteen inches away, you got serious problems...."

This indicates there are rule book definitions of various facets of the game such as the strike zone and the reality of the game with, for instance, some umps having generous strike zones, extending beyond the limits in the written rules.

(6) Yes, this will undoubtedly be called a double play. The second base man was in the vicinity, or "neighborhood," of the bag so the umpire will say he recorded the force play even though he really wasn't on or in contact with the bag while he was in possession of the ball. Obviously, if umpires strictly enforced the rules 100 percent of the time, Sizemore would be safe at second. This is known as the "phantom" double play and baseball people are willing to go along with their rules being stretched a bit as long as such calls go both ways.

It's much like players' reactions to umpires whose strike zones don't fully adhere to the rule book. "As long as an umpire establishes his strike zone early on in games and remains consistent all day, that's fine," they generously say. In this instance, because the umpires are protecting middle infielders on all clubs by "giving" them the force on close plays, managers usually don't gripe about the phantom tag of the bag.

Make no mistake, middle infielders do need protection with rugged runners, often wearing metal spikes capable of slashing flesh, setting sights on them around the bag. Former second baseman Junior Spivey showed one writer his legs which, even though he had played only a few seasons, were spiderwebbed with scars.

Final note: Bill Veeck once suggested the real reason the phantom out at second came to be practiced by umpires was that by giving anything close to the defense on a consistent basis, umps could minimize controversy over many too-close-to-call force plays around second base.

(7) If a ball hits in foul territory, say behind the plate, then the spin on the ball forces the ball into fair territory, the ball is live and fair so Tracy would be out.

(8) Because the ball touched the batter while he was in the box and in foul territory, it is foul and is instantly dead.

(9) Here, because the ball struck the batter while he was in fair territory and considered to be out of the batter's box, he is automatically out.

(10) Once the catcher, intentionally or otherwise, touched home plate while in possession of the ball, the runner from third is out on this force play and the batter is free to make his way to first. When the dust settled, the runner from second scored and men were on second and third with two outs.

(11) No, the run does not score on a simple out at first (or any force play) to end an inning.

(12) This is indeed a different situation than in the previous question. Here the runner, Ramirez, gets rewarded for his hustle—he scored before Cantu was retired stretching his hit and there was certainly no force on him as he tried for second voluntarily. Had Ramirez loafed and not crossed home before the out, his run would have been waved off.

(13) Most umpires will tell you that players are given leeway when it comes to routine grumbling. Usually a player won't get ejected for swearing or, in general, fuming over a call. In fact, using the so-called Queen Mother of swear words is permitted. However, when a player's comments or cursing get personal—such as sticking the word "you"

after the using the "biggie"—he will almost invariably be instructed to hit the showers—he's through for the day.

Umpire Fieldin Culbreth, a veteran of more than thirteen big league seasons, explained that if a player shouts out that he made a terrible call, he can live with that. If, however, the player had personalized it by saying, "*You're* terrible," (or worse) then it's time to give him the thumb.

Some actions, such as the time back on September 27, 1996, when Robbie Alomar spit on plate umpire John Hirschbeck after being called out on strikes, will not only get a player kicked out of a game, but draw a serious fine and/or suspension as well.

Brett Locher, an amateur umpire, met big league ump Vic Voltaggio in the 1980s when Voltaggio was just coming off a series in Detroit, working a game when Sparky Anderson was managing the Tigers. "On the front page of the *Detroit Free Press* at that time," said Locher, "they had [a photo of] Voltaggio giving the big gesture to throw Anderson out of the game. I asked him at that level what do they say, because usually it takes the magic word, [to get thumbed]. I asked him, 'What was the magic word in this case?' He said, 'Sparky came out and said that I had been screwing him pretty much all game long,' and he kept [repeating] that many, many times. Then Voltaggio says, 'Then this time I'm really gonna screw you,' and he tossed him out of the game." Clearly, each ump has his own limits, his boiling point.

Locher also recalled a time when Earl Weaver, famous for his run-ins with Ron Luciano, was angry with his old nemesis from a previous game. Before the next contest began Weaver strolled to home plate holding a copy of the rule book. "He ripped it up right in front of Luciano and said, 'Seeing how you make up your own rules, Ron, I guess we don't need this book anymore.' He threw Weaver out before the game even started." Weaver once did a variation of those actions, burying the rule book near home plate.

On August 23, 1952, Augie Donatelli thumbed Bob Elliott of the New York Giants for arguing a called strike and for kicking dirt on the man in blue. Bobby Hoffman replaced Elliott in the box, inheriting the count. When he was rung up on strikes he argued so vociferously he, too, got the thumb—two men ejected over one at bat.

Once venerable ump Al Barlick, a Hall of Famer, called an inside pitch a strike on the Braves' Johnny Logan. Barlick was famous for his impartiality, having once stated, "On a close pitch, the hitter wants it, the pitcher wants it. I don't care who gets it." Logan certainly wanted the call that day. To show his displeasure he left the batter's box and used the knob end of the bat to draw a line in the dirt to indicate where the last pitch had traveled—very clearly, he believed, off the plate. The unflappable Barlick then took the bat away from Logan and did his own scrawling in the dirt: "$50 Fine."

Lou Piniella was known to unanchor and heave a base or two in a fury. Of course the repercussion of such behavior is inevitable: toss a bag, get tossed.

Former minor league umpire Homer "Duke" Rash remembered a day when a pitcher's control was off, "and he was thinking that I was missing the calls. The ball was thrown back out to the pitcher and I came around to sweep off home plate. When I straightened up, he threw the ball and hit me in the middle of the back." His partner that day, Bruce Froemming, immediately ejected the pitcher, a no-brainer decision. Naturally such actions and others such as throwing equipment and poking or bumping an umpire are never tolerated.

Well, *almost* never. Umpires sometimes choose to pretend they didn't see, hear, or even feel some things. They, not unlike policemen, can choose to ignore slight violations and, instead of doling out punishment, can issue warnings or completely look the other way. One-time minor league umpire Ed Rogers said, "In the heated argument, contact will be made, but a bump is willful and deliberate contact and definitely will not be tolerated—he'll be ejected immediately." So there's a line between touching and bumping, a very important distinction.

His partner, Tyler Bolick, explained, "Sometimes contact occurs and it isn't considered a bump, so we don't report it. Each case [that is reported] is an individual one that the league president decides."

By the way, one of the most famous ejections, certainly one which led to a most improbable outcome took place on June 23, 1917, when the game's starting pitcher, none other than Boston's Babe Ruth, began arguing with home plate umpire Brick Owens from the first pitch of the contest. After Owens called the first four pitches balls, Ruth was boiling, a cauldron of uncontrolled anger. Convinced that three of the pitches were strikes, Ruth stated, "When he called the fourth one on me, I just went crazy."

Warned that he was about to get ejected, Ruth threatened to hit Owens if he tossed him. Owens followed through and so did Ruth, firing a punch which landed for a strike directly on his jaw. Ruth had to be escorted off the field by a police officer. The Bambino was replaced by Ernie Shore, who then mowed down twenty-seven consecutive Washington Senators to record the fourth perfect game in baseball history and, as would be expected, the only one ever to involve a relief pitcher. Ruth would be fined (though only a $100 love tap on his wrist) and he was suspended for ten days.

(14) By rule Gant was safe, but umpire Drew Coble, perhaps screened by Hrbek on the play, must have felt Gant slipped off the bag on his own and not because of the tag by Hrbek. Gant, despite the rhubarb that quickly ensued, was out.

Gant would gain fame later in the Series when, in Game Seven, he scored the run on a tenth-inning pinch hit by Gene Larkin to clinch the World Championship for the Twins. That was the classic contest in which Jack Morris toughed it out for all ten innings, refusing to give the ball up, throwing 126 pitches (79 for strikes) en route to his eight-strikeout win.

(15) Umpires can distinguish the difference between the sound of a runner's foot coming down sharply on first base and the noise the ball makes as it thumps into the first baseman's mitt. Often that is the only way for him to make up his mind between making a safe or an out call. Remember, contrary to the belief of many amateur players, officially there is no rule stating a tie goes to the runner. The rules simply say a runner is safe if he gets to the bag before the ball does and while, in reality, there *can* be ties on photo-finish plays, umps must rule one way or the other.

(16) It's a fair ball. The plate is in fair territory.

(17) Sure, what Posada did is a wise, routine play, a simple force play at the plate, and the Jays come up empty-handed.

(18) The move by Lopez certainly was not kosher. It was a case of obstruction. Lopez was charged with an error, Crawford was awarded home, and the game ended with a Tampa Bay victory.

(19) Any time a hitter bunts the ball foul with two strikes, it counts as a strikeout. However, at one time there was no rule prohibiting such an action. One story attributed the origin of this rule to Anson, who played from 1871 through 1897, hitting a crisp .333 lifetime. He had such great bat control he could intentionally bunt countless pitches foul. While he may have gained an advantage by wearing out pitchers,

his tactic slowed the game down and any time one of his bunts was popped foul into the stands more than one miserly team owner cringed at the prospect of having to replace those balls.

20 Conlan waved off the run, citing the rule which indicates a runner must touch home plate before, in this case, Reiser was retired for the inning-ending out. Had Reiser got caught in a run down, giving Bragan time to score, the run would have counted.

21 If you declared Sewell's play illegal, give yourself credit for a correct answer even though, at the time, there was nothing in the rule book to ban his actions. Thus, in reality, Fonseca's hit was taken away from him, and he had to reenter the batter's box, where he whiffed on the next pitch. According to Sewell, a new rule was drawn up overnight to stop such shenanigans.

22 Yes, Bragan's using nine consecutive pinch hitters is legal, but it certainly depleted his bench and handcuffed further maneuvering. In addition, the league's commissioner could well have fined Bragan had he felt he was making a travesty of the game.

23 No, it certainly isn't kosher. Bragan confirmed he knew he was pulling a quick one when he stated, "I never had the guts to do it in a regular [season] game, only in spring training."

Bragan, seemingly a precursor to colorful skippers such as Earl Weaver and Lou Piniella, once pleaded with an umpire to ask for help on a call he had just made. When the ump refused, the irate Bragan said, "You telling me you're God, is that right? He said, 'That's right,' and I said, 'Well, I'm going to lie down and worship at your feet.'" He then assumed that position while a *Life* magazine photographer captured one of the funnier demonstrative managerial protests ever.

(24) Although Crisp felt the seagull interfered with him, so to speak, costing him a chance to make a play on DeRosa at the plate, the ball is alive. It remained in play, and the run counted (there was a trailing runner, but in this situation his presence was moot). It was certainly a very odd way to end a ball game—for Choo, a walk off hit, for the seagull, a fly-off escape from what could have been a serious injury.

The next game, Indians' officials, well aware of the nuisance created by the flock of seagulls, decided to discourage their presence. At the end of every half inning a salvo of fireworks was set off to frighten them away—the move seemed to work and that contest featured no strange plays.

(25) Harris was instructed to advance two bases as the penalty for Bradley's throw which traveled out of play and into the stands. Cubs fans erupted into a mighty volley of boos—the fact that even after Bradley went 2-for-4 on the day (he was still hitting only .224

on the year) didn't help matters. His defensive lapse was a situation which some felt was akin to a Manny Ramirez "Manny being Manny" moment, with the name "Milton" replacing "Manny" here.

The incident was also reminiscent of the famous misplay when Larry Walker of the Montreal Expos was patrolling right field one day against the Dodgers. He, too, lost track of the number of outs and after he caught a fly ball off Mike Piazza's bat near the stands, he handed the ball to a young fan in the first row of the seats and was about to make his way to his dugout. Then, realizing his faux pas, he retrieved the ball from the boy and fired it back into the infield—too late, like Bradley, his boneheaded play cost his team. The runner, Jose Offerman, tagged on the play but that was unnecessary. Once the ball left the playing field Offerman had third base automatically. Walker later joked, "I get a lot of people asking me for balls now."

In a case of history repeating itself *and* of people not learning from history, on September 10, 1998, Derek Bell of the Houston Astros caught a fly ball off the bat of Marquis Grissom and, thinking it was out number three, he, too, lobbed a live ball into the stands, giving a runner off first two free bases.

(26) Given the circumstances of the play as told by Hemus, Throneberry would get credit only for a single.

Hemus recalled that one run was allowed to score and that the umpire Stengel was arguing with warned him, "If you don't get out of here and [the Cubs] throw to first base [for an appeal there], you're not going to get any runs at all. He missed first *and* second."

Throneberry was the poster boy for the woeful, bungling Mets. That season he played 116 games, and hit .244 with sixteen homers and only fourty nine runs batted in. In just ninety-seven games at first base he committed an ungodly seventeen errors. Sportswriter Jimmy Breslin once said, "Having Marv Throneberry play for your team is like having [notorious stick-up artist] Willie Sutton play for your bank."

It should be noted that numerous other accounts of this tale exist. One says it was one of Stengel's coaches who calmed the manager down by saying, "Don't bother arguing, Casey. He missed first base, too." Another mentions no base runners other than Throneberry being involved on the play. The batter after Throneberry, Charlie Neal, homered, which caused Stengel to catapult out of his dugout and point at each of the bases so Neal was sure not to pull a Throneberry and miss a base (or two). Had Throneberry not been called out, he would have scored on the homer which later became vital in the game won by a scant 8–7 margin by the Cubs.

Final note: Baseball lore does not always get all the facts straight. The impeccable Web site baseball-reference.com states Throneberry, credited with a single, did drive home both Woodling and Thomas.

At any rate, the penalty is the same for missing a base regardless of all the variations on the Throneberry scenario—you are out and you go back to the dugout.

27 Basically, no. The Cardinals were positive it was a horrendous call, but all they could do was gripe. By the time the dust settled, home plate umpire Augie Donatelli gave the boot to both Solly Hemus and Eddie Stanky. With great equanimity, Musial finally stepped back in the box and doubled to right. That triggered a six-run inning and the Cards went on to win.

28 The contact between Jones's bat and the head gear of Rodriguez is immaterial (except for the pain "Pudge" would feel). The ball is alive and the hit stands.

29 Berkman is permitted to try for first and if McCann (or someone on defense) doesn't retrieve and fire the ball there before Berkman hits the bag, he is safe.

30 Under the circumstances in this question, Berkman is not allowed to make his way to first base as it was already occupied at the time of his third strike.

31 With two men out, the rule states that even if first base is occupied, Berkman is still entitled to try for first. This is a commonly misunderstood rule at lower levels of baseball, but it boils down to this: With two men out *or* with first base unoccupied in any situation, a batter is permitted to try to reach first if the third strike is not cleanly fielded;

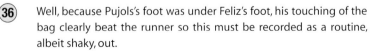

with less than two men out the batter can try for first only if there wasn't a runner there when the strikeout took place.

 32 The umpires can only report such actions. When Bob Watson, Major League Baseball's vice president in charge of discipline, learned what Trembley had done, he suspended him for two days and fined him.

 33 The correct ruling is to allow the base runner one base and declare the ball to be dead.

 34 No catcher's balk here—Varitek followed the proper procedure perfectly for an intentional walk by standing inside the box until the ball left his pitcher's hand.

35 This one is the old "when is a catch not a catch" issue. By definition, in order for it to be considered a catch, the fielder has to have total control of both the ball—he must truly possess, *control* the ball—and his body. In this question the ruling would be no catch, just a long foul ball.

36 Well, because Pujols's foot was under Feliz's foot, his touching of the bag clearly beat the runner so this must be recorded as a routine, albeit shaky, out.

37 The ball, according to the clues given, hit well beyond the bag before it caromed into foul grounds so it is a fair ball. A catalyst, Furcal got the first hit of five in a four-run first inning of a Dodgers' 7–5 victory—and it came on a very peculiar hit, a bunt double.

38 A player can't *call* time out, he can only *request* it—an umpire must declare that time is out. If the home plate ump feels the hitter asked for a time out when the pitcher was about to release the ball, he won't grant the request. Valbuena knew that and, not hearing the umpire call, "Time out," jumped back into his hitting position just in case.

   If a player could call for time whenever he felt like it, the game would change drastically. Remember the time big Willie Stargell, known for his towering home runs and most certainly *not* for his speed, was running on the pitch (hopefully on a hit and run and not a straight steal) and had managed only to lumber about two-thirds of the way to second base when it was obvious that he was about to be thrown out. The Pirates star, in a moment of whimsy, signaled for a time out.

39 The ball is foul and is immediately dead upon touching the batter.

40 In this case, with Mantle out of the batter's box and in fair territory, the situation is very different. In fact, he must be declared out and the ball is dead. If there was anybody on base, they are frozen where they were at the time of the pitch.

(41) This should be a rather routine one. Because nobody called time, the ball is naturally alive so the runners' advancements on the base paths count. Astros manager Cecil Cooper immediately lifted the mortified Hampton and the Dodgers went on to win easily, 5–2. After the contest Hampton explained that he thought the home plate ump had called time out just after Blake had slid home.

(42) Foucault said of the cheap beer night debacle in Cleveland: "It finally got so horrendous on the field that Nestor Chylak just called the game off." Naturally, the umpires forfeited the game to the visitors. In a forfeited game the official score is listed as 9–0. Such games are so rare veteran umpires Fieldin Culbreth and Bruce Froemming (who worked more games than any umpire save Bill Klem) said they've never been a part of one. "The closest I ever came to anything like that was clearing the bench and that happened a couple of times," Froemming said, "but never a situation where you're going to forfeit a game."

Bruce Doane stated, "I forfeited a game one time when I was very, very young when a manager for a Division III school sat on the mound and would not leave after I threw him out of the game. I said,

'I'm pretty much giving you about one minute here. If you don't get up and go, I'm going to go.' And that's what happened."

Forfeits have been extremely rare in recent years. Aside from the two already mentioned, only three others have taken place since way back in 1954. One came in 1971, when a forfeit was awarded to the Yankees when the Senators, playing in their last game ever in Washington (the team would move to Texas and become the Rangers the following season), could not control the crowd which, with two outs in the final inning, mobbed the field seeking souvenirs.

Another one happened in mid-September 1977 when Marty Springstead told Baltimore manager Earl Weaver that he refused his request to remove a tarpaulin which covered the Toronto bullpen. Weaver felt the slippery surface could come into play and perhaps lead to an injury to his left fielder. Angry over Springstead's decision, Weaver yanked his team from the field and, fifteen minutes later, the game was forfeited.

The fifth forfeit since '54 was the last forfeit ever to take place in the National League in more than forty years and remains the last one ever in the majors. That one occurred on August 10, 1995, in Los Angeles. The chaos took place when the Dodgers hosted a Ball Night. In the bottom of the seventh, fans pelted the field with the give-away balls. Two innings later after an argument, which ultimately led to two ejections, broke out over a ball-strike call (Raul Mondesi was called out looking), fans again bombarded the diamond, this time with about 200 baseballs, and umpires ordered the visiting Cardinals into the dugout for their own protection. Shortly after, when play resumed, a warning of an impending forfeit was issued over the public-address system, but more balls showered down, one nearly hitting St. Louis outfielder Brian Jordan. That did it; the umps awarded the Cards the win.

(43) Froemming called a double play. He said, "I took the runs off the board. I was a rookie umpire and when you're a rookie umpire with that type of a call, an interference call, you don't have any credibility to go back on with the manager and the players . . . so the argument was the biggest argument I ever had—it was fourteen minutes and four guys got chased, and I had the play right. It just shows you, you can have a play right and it doesn't matter because when they think they're right, they [go] crazy on us. That'd be the biggest play I ever had and the longest argument I ever had."

ICHIRO SUZUKI

BASIC SITUATIONS

In this section of the book the plays and situations you will cope with are ones that come up, perhaps not too often, but certainly from time to time during games. For example, catcher's interference and even fan interference are dealt with here in Section Two.

For decades umpires have been taught that, even when they are a bit unsure of their call—say, on a play in which the runner *may* have beat a throw to first base by a micro-second—the authoritative thing to do, the thing an umpire *must* do to keep his reputation as the man who is running the show, is to make the call quickly and forcefully. Sell your call—let everyone watching know that you are *certain* you are in the right. And, face it, even if your missed the ultra-close call, you *are* correct; in that your call will stand.

Here, then, are situations requiring you to take everything into consideration and then make your call assuredly. Of course, in your case you can always peek in the answers section to insure you are correct. For that matter, because you are not held to the strict scrutiny umpires are subjected to, you can sneak a look at the answers and, if need be, change your call. At any rate, read on and good luck.

◊ ◊ ◊

YOU'RE THE UMPIRE

(1) On the Fourth of July during America's bicentennial year, Philadelphia Phillies catcher Tim McCarver "celebrated" the occasion by hitting a home run (in fact, a grand slam) which turned out *not* to be a homer.

It all began when Greg Luzinski faced the Pittsburgh Pirates to open the second inning of the first game of a double header. "The Bull" drove a Larry Demery pitch to the opposite field and lumbered into third base with a leadoff triple. Dick Allen followed and drew a walk before Jay Johnstone doubled to center field, scoring Luzinski for the game's first run and sending Allen scampering into third base.

At that point Pirates manager Danny Murtaugh ordered an intentional walk be issued to Garry Maddox to load the bases, setting up a force play at any base, in hopes of turning a double play. Sure, another run would score on the DP—barring, say, one of the third baseman to the catcher and on to the first baseman variety— but it was still early in the game and a 2–0 deficit with two outs seemed like a manageable situation, especially since a double play would result in the Pirates needing only one more out in order to get out of the mess. Plus the next hitter due after the hoped-for twin killing would be the opposing pitcher.

Then it happened. McCarver belted a long drive to right field. The ball towered high in the air, so McCarver was unsure as to whether it would leave the park or not. Therefore, he kept his eyes on the path of the ball and not on his destination as he scooted down the line. Now, the Philly runner off first, Maddox, was also uncertain about the fly ball's final landing spot. "Would it," he wondered, "be caught?" If so, he figured, he couldn't drift too far from first base. The moment McCarver saw the ball clear the wall, he dashed around first and, in the process, also went past Maddox.

If you were the umpire and spotted this infraction of the rules, what would your call be?

Answer on pages 85–86

(2) On October 9, 1996, the Baltimore Orioles and the New York Yankees were battling in Game One of the American League Championship Series. In the bottom half of the eighth inning, with the O's up 4–3, Yankee shortstop Derek Jeter launched an Armando Benitez pitch, lifting it toward the stands in right field. It appeared that the ball would come down just shy of the fence when, suddenly, two small hands reached over the fence and made contact with the ball, which then was deflected into the seats. The hands belonged not to a player, but to Jeffrey Maier, a twelve-year-old Yankees fan seated in the first row of seats by the wall. Orioles outfielder Tony Tarasco and his manager, Davey Johnson, erupted with near-volcanic force. "I could have made the catch," he contended moments before umpires huddled. What's the ruling here? Was it a game-tying, solo home run or if Tarasco's contention was right, should Jeter be declared out?

Answer on page 86

3 The next play is similar but involves a fan touching a ball in foul territory, not fair ground. In 2003, when the Chicago Cubs were seemingly about to nail down a win which would propel them into the World Series, the Wrigley Field roof fell in on them. Leading the Florida Marlins 3–0 in Game Six of the National League Championship Series, the Cubs needed just five outs to wrap up the NL pennant for the first time since 1945. Mark Prior was breezing along on a three-hitter. Florida's speedy Juan Pierre was on second base, having doubled to left with one out, and Luis Castillo was at the plate.

It was then that a fan by the name of Steve Bartman did something which led to October 14, 2003, becoming a day of infamy in Chicagoland.

When a foul fly ball approached him, he instinctively reached for his potential souvenir. However, left fielder Moises Alou was also in pursuit of the ball, seconds away from securing it. Reaching into the stands, Alou jumped and stabbed for the ball only to be thwarted when Bartman made contact with it. A frustrated Alou slammed his glove in anger as umpire Mike Everitt called out "no catch." But hold on a second. Could Cubs manager Dusty Baker appeal to the umpires and ask for a call of fan interference, pleading that an automatic out be awarded to the Cubs?

Answer on pages **87–89**

4 Paul Richards managed the Chicago White Sox from 1951 through most of the 1954 season. He was a man with a mind as sharp as the literal definition of his highly unusual middle name, Rapier. Richards is credited with many innovations and it is believed he was the first skipper to come up with a ploy whose legality you'll be asked to consider.

Richards had starting pitcher Billy Pierce, a lefty, on the mound when the opposition sent a right-handed hitter to the plate. Richards wanted to bring in a righty reliever to retire the batter, given the righty-on-righty advantage in that scenario. However, Richards also wanted his starter to remain in the game. Is there any way he can have it both ways? Was he able to manipulate the rule books and thus skirt intervention by the umpires?

Answer on page **89**

(5) Some situations are very rare yet the call should be relatively simple. For example, when the Cleveland Indians played host to the Texas Rangers on May 26, 1993, Jose Canseco made the blooper hall of shame when he tried to corral a fly ball off the bat of Cleveland's Carlos Martinez. Canseco, the Texas right fielder that day, butchered the play from the start, pirouetting back toward the ball. To make matters far worse, he gauged its flight so badly that the ball bounced off his head and over the wall—it was as if Canseco had performed a soccer "header." Unable to track the ball properly, he had become as disoriented as a shanghaied sailor (and he soon became just as dazed). Was this a home run?

Answer on page **90**

6 The next real life play in question is rather the opposite side of the Canseco coin. Rodney McCray valiantly tried to make a sensational catch on a ball, one that didn't go over the fence; but on this play the defender actually went *through* the wall.

It all began as McCray's Triple-A Vancouver Canadians of the Pacific Coast League traveled to Civic Stadium in Portland, Oregon, on May 27, 1991. Chip Hale of the Portland Beavers drove the ball deep into the outfield where McCray tried to chase it down in right field, near the 369-foot marker on the wall.

Now, McCray nearly made a play as breathtaking as a circus high wire act, but he did not make the catch (the ball hit off the wall), nor could he put on his brakes in time—so he crashed *through* the plywood fence in one of baseball's most memorable moments. Had he made the catch, would it have counted? Or, since McCray would have left the field of play with the ball secured on his person, so to speak, is it a rule book double or perhaps a homer?

Answer on pages **90–92**

7 Los Angeles Dodgers pitcher Don Drysdale was talented enough to be the ace of most any pitching staff. However, with the Dodgers, for several years he was relegated to being their second-best hurler, behind the great Sandy Koufax.

In 1968, however, he did something that topped every other pitcher in the history of the game to that point. He threw

$58\frac{2}{3}$ consecutive shutout innings. His remarkable run began on with four straight shutouts: on May 14 he toiled for a 1–0 win, topping future Hall of Famer Fergie Jenkins; four days later he won his third 1–0 contest of the year—as well as he was pitching (his ERA at the end of the day was a microscopic 1.85), his record then stood at a modest 3–3; on May 22, he came back with a 2–0 victory over another future Hall of Famer, Bob Gibson; he finally got a bit of run support in his 5–0 shutout on May 26, though even then his Dodger teammates had backed him up with just two runs through the first seven innings.

Then, on the final day in May, now sporting a 5–3 record with a sparkling 1.47 ERA, he faced the rival San Francisco Giants. He took his shutout streak into the top of the ninth inning when danger struck. With two men out and Giants on every base (via a walk to Willie McCovey, a single by Jim Ray Hart, and a walk to Dave Marshall), "Double D" ran the count to 2–2 against Dick Dietz. The next pitch trailed inside and hit Dietz, who stood still, allowing the ball to hit him. That action, or lack of action, forced in a run, halting Drysdale's shutout string—or did it? What is the correct call here?

Answer on pages **92–94**

(8) The date was October 10, 1970, and the occasion was Game One of the World Series in Cincinnati's Riverfront Stadium. In the sixth inning of a 3–3 ball game, the Reds had Tommy Helms on first base and Bernie Carbo at third with one out against the Baltimore Orioles.

Ty Cline stepped up as a pinch hitter for Woody Woodward to face Jim Palmer, a future Hall of Famer. Cline hit a Baltimore chop, perhaps fifteen feet in the air, just in front of the plate where catcher Elrod Hendricks finally pounced upon the ball. Home plate ump Ken Burkhart came out of his crouch and stood with his feet on either side of the third base line, ruling the ball was fair.

It was then that Hendricks decided his play was not on Cline going to first, but on Carbo coming down the line. Meanwhile, Carbo's slide hooked around Burkhart's feet, causing him to hit the dirt, a position from which no ump wants to make a call—especially this one, a crucial decision during the World Series.

Hendricks then tagged Carbo as Burkhart was hitting the deck. However, the catcher applied the tag with his mitt *but* the ball was in his right hand. One more thing—Carbo never touched the plate! Not seeing all of that action transpire, the umpire made what he felt (based on what he saw) was an honest call: He declared Carbo out. How did this mess get sorted out?

Answer on page **94**

(9) The play which follows is seldom seen in the majors because at that level all the players know the rule which applies in this situation. Still, it's one which is often botched at the low amateur levels.

A batter hits a grounder to third and, hustling hard down the line, beats it out for an infield hit. His hustle to first took him beyond the bag, several yards down the line. When he turns casually to his left, to make a 180-degree turn to return to his base, the first baseman applies a tag to him, informing the umpire that the runner had made a move to second base, thus giving up his right to overrun first. Is the runner out or safe?

Answer on pages **94–95**

(10) Tom Paciorek was with the Seattle Mariners when his M's took on the Oakland A's. Billy Martin, manager of the A's, called "time out," approached the home plate umpire, and contended Paciorek was outside the batter's box—or at least he was outside what should have been chalked off as the box. In other words, Martin argued the box was larger than the rules allow. If you were working the plate, what would you do?

Answer on page **95**

(11) When the Detroit Tigers hosted the New York Yankees on June 28, 1976, crowd of nearly 50,000 turned out to see Detroit's rookie sensation Mark "The Bird" Fidrych try to boost his record to 8–1. Early in the game Ron LeFlore faced Yankees pitcher Ken Holtzman and starched a 2–2 pitch, hitting a high hopper down the third base line. In fact, the ball struck the front of the bag, just on the corner which nestled next to the foul line, and forcefully deflected directly to the Tigers' third base coach Joe Schultz. After hitting him, the ball died near the

coaching box. Veteran announcers Bob Prince and Bob Uecker stated they had never seen such a play occur. Third base umpire Russ Goetz may or may not have seen it before, but he immediately knew what to call—what did he rule?

Answer on pages **95–96**

(12) This play should never occur in the majors but happens fairly often at the much lower levels of the game. The batter hits a slow four-hopper to the shortstop whose hurried throw pulls the first baseman off the bag. At that same time, the batter misses the bag as he runs down the line. What should the first base umpire do? What does he signal?

Answer on page **96**

(13) In the first of two All-Star games in 1961, this one on July 11 in San Francisco's blustery Candlestick Park, the diminutive Stu Miller was on the mound for the National League when a strange play, still legendary today, took place. The NL led 3–1 entering the top of the ninth. With one out Al Kaline drove home Nellie Fox on a single, then advanced to second on a Roger Maris base hit. That is when it happened.

"The wind blew me about a half an inch or so," Miller recalled, "and I kind of weaved." He did not, he insisted, fall off the mound as baseball lore has it, but the key is he did move while on the rubber? What call is the correct one here?

Answer on pages **96–97**

BASIC SITUATIONS

(14) The Los Angeles Dodgers and the New York Yankees played in a coast-to-coast World Series back in 1978. On October 14, during Game Four, controversial, colorful Reggie Jackson once more found himself in the middle of a maelstrom. Leading by a score of 3–1 in the sixth inning, the Dodgers were sitting pretty. With Yankee outfielder Lou Piniella at the plate, Thurman Munson at second, and Jackson leading off first with one out, the Dodgers were thinking double play. Piniella obliged by hitting a tailor-made D.P. ball to shortstop Bill Russell, who spiked the bag at second for a force out then threw to first to complete the twin killing.

Realizing his team's plight, Jackson thrust his right hip into the path of the ball, thus sending it off its course and into right field. Munson scored and Piniella reached safely. If you had been working this game what call would you have made?

Answer on pages **97–98**

(15) Let's say it's 2008 and Detroit Tigers manager Jim Leyland feels it is time for his starting pitcher, Justin Verlander, to depart as he was tiring and had allowed Oakland A's batters to fill the bases. Leyland brings in Casey Fossum, a lefty, to face a right-handed hitter for the A's. At that point Oakland's skipper, Bob Geren, sends right-handed hitting Mike Sweeney to the plate as a pinch hitter. Can Leyland now decide to dip into his bullpen once again and replace Fossum with a right-handed pitcher to gain an advantage over the A's? And if he

can, what's to prevent Geren with going to his bench and sending another lefty to the plate? Explain the rule involved here.

Answer on page **98**

(16) Back on August 29, 1992, Atlanta pitcher Charlie Leibrandt secured his thousand career strikeout. He wanted to keep the ball as a trophy, so he rolled it to a teammate in his club's dugout. However, in the happiness of the moment, Leibrandt had neglected to call time out. Did the umps permit Ricky Jordan, the only base runner at the time to advance? If so, how many bases?

Answer on page **99**

(17) Imagine it's the twilight of the career of the great graybeard Gaylord Perry, notorious for loading a ball up, for throwing a "wet one." Frequently he would make gestures such as touching the bill of his cap or wiping the hair near his right ear to make batters suspect he had a foreign substance such as Vaseline cached there. Convinced, that the next pitch was a loaded one, hitters were often agitated, off stride, and, quite often, fooled. That was Perry's trick—sometimes he would throw a spit ball, but other times his actions were a mere decoy.

Now, in this scenario, he is on the rubber and really wants to play cat and mouse with the batter, so he puts his fingers up to his mouth, doesn't really lick them, but then pretends to wipe excess spit off on his uniform pants. Has he done something wrong among all those gyrations? If so, what?

Answer on pages **99–101**

(18) One key to the next question is the time frame, the mid-1960s. Here's your problem: Prior to a game between the San Francisco Giants and the Los Angeles Dodgers the ebullient Willie Mays spots a former teammate, now with the Dodgers, standing near the batting cage. Mays strolls over to his old friend and strikes up a conversation about the old days and about hitting. Has he possibly violated a rule?

Answer on pages **101–102**

(19) It's an hour before the scheduled first pitch, but a storm rolls in and saturates the field. Nearing game time the deluge has tapered off to a drizzle. Should the game be started or not? When it comes to calling off or delaying the start of a game due to adverse conditions before the contest has already started, before the umps have been given both teams' lineup cards, who is in control?

Answer on pages **102–106**

(20) In the 1950s a strange, yet heads-up play took place at Ebbets Field when the Dodgers had runners on first (Junior Gilliam) and second (Don Hoak). The batter hit a grounder to short which appeared to be a guaranteed double play. Suddenly, the cunning Hoak grabbed the

ball with his bare hand, then dropped it. He was ruled out on the spot, but had cleverly avoided a D.P.—or did he? For that matter, could he argue that by rule a runner hit by a batted ball is out, but the batter is awarded a single?

Answer on page **107**

(21) Another situation from the 1950s: The Phillies' Andy Seminick was at the plate in a game against the New York Giants when second baseman Eddie Stanky, a well-known agitator, positioned himself well to the right of where he normally played, in direct line with home plate and the pitcher. He began jumping up and down, waving his arms as if he were performing side straddle hops. Clearly he was trying to distract Seminick. Was he committing an illegal act?

Answer on page **107**

(22) Bobby Bragan holds the distinction of having been the oldest professional baseball manager—as well as the oldest one to get ejected. Bragan was inserted into a minor league game as a manager with the sole purpose of topping Connie Mack, by a scant week, as the oldest manager ever. John Dittrich became president of the Fort Worth Cats of an independent league, Bragan recounted, and "it was his idea that I manage that team for one night." That evening Bragan—at the age of eighty-seven years, nine months, and sixteen days—got ejected from a professional baseball game, and *that*, he related, was no stunt.

"I did it because the shortstop was ejected in the third inning—the umpire threw him out on strike three before he ever left home plate, [he was] still in the batter's box." Bragan said the batter hardly had the chance to say or do anything before he was tossed. In fact he got only one sentence out of his mouth—that was *it*.

"I just automatically got up and walked out to him. I said, 'That's the only time I've ever seen a man get thrown out that quickly, from the batter's box—did he call you a dirty name?' He said, 'No, he didn't.' I said, 'Did he use profanity?' He said, 'No, he didn't.' I said, 'What'd he say?' He said, '[The batter] said I was doing a lousy job.' I said, 'Well, I'll go along with that.' He said, 'You go with him.' Isn't that something?"

True to the managerial code, Bragan added, "Anyway, we won the game, 11–10."

In any event, Bragan said he still remembers one game between his Milwaukee Braves and the St. Louis Cardinals featuring an odd play which unfolded when Hank Aaron was at the plate and Curt Simmons was on the hill. "Simmons was a slow ball pitcher—threw a lot of change of paces—and he threw one to Hank and he took an extra step, moved his right foot forward a little bit and his left foot forward, and he hit one over the right field wall." After Aaron's fancy dance steps, one foot was out of the batter's box. Did this make, by the rule book's definition, Aaron himself out of the box? What would the punishment be if he was indeed considered to be outside of the batter's box?

Answer on pages **107–108**

(23) Speaking of ejections, here's a strange one. On May 16, 2009, Angels starting pitcher John Lackey was making his first start of the year after opening the season on the disabled list. His first pitch buzzed Texas Rangers second baseman Ian Kinsler, with the ball's path actually going behind his head, a serious and dangerous breech of the pitching code. Kinsler had swatted two home runs the night before, so Lackey's intent seemed obvious—he was sending the old message, "Don't dig in, don't get too comfortable at the plate against us."

Lackey's next pitch, another high one, hit Kinsler in his torso prompting home plate ump Bob Davidson to thumb Lackey, whose season through mid-May now consisted of two pitches. Lackey, according to reports of the game, "raised his arms on the mound with a look of disbelief on his face."

Was he correct to be so outraged? According to the rules, would the ejection stand? Can an umpire toss a player without first issuing a warning to him and his team?

Answer on page **109**

(24) When the Cleveland Indians traveled to Cincinnati for interleague play in May 2009, an obstruction play took place. Grady Sizemore had tripled to right, with the ball traveling into the corner. As he slid into third, Jerry Hairston Jr.'s throw eluded Adam Rosales. Sizemore alertly jumped up and jetted toward the plate, but not before Rosales hindered Sizemore's advance. Sizemore then raced home while left fielder Jonny Gomes, backing up the play, fired the ball to catcher Ryan Hanigan. As the dust cleared, home plate ump Mark Wegner called Sizemore out.

Rosales stated truthfully that Sizemore "didn't even graze me." The Indians' star outfielder concurred. "We didn't necessarily run into each other. He was more in my path. I hesitated, but I was surprised he called it." Now, given what the two principles involved in the play testified, did Wegner make the right call?

Answer on page **109**

(25) Back on May 10, 1997, the Chicago Cubs turned in an odd play due to the blustery conditions in the Windy City. It began when a pop up was hit into shallow center field. Cub infielder Shawon Dunston went back for the ball and the umpires invoked the infield fly rule.

However, Dunston fought the stiff breeze and lost the battle, and the ball fell in. Two runners then tried to advance but both were gunned down. What's the ruling here? Send the runners back because the ball should be dead or call them out?

Answer on page **109**

(26) On September 15, 1993, star pitcher Orel Hershiser's name was on the starting lineup card as the third baseman hitting in the number three slot. His Dodgers were on the road so Los Angeles came to the plate first. When it was Hershiser's turn to bat, he was lifted for a pinch hitter. Thus, even though his name intentionally appeared on the lineup card, the move seemed inexplicable as he was never used in the game in any capacity. Is such a move proper?

Answer on pages **109–110**

(27) The next play doesn't happen too often in the majors, but it's a rather tough call for casual fans. The year is 2004. Imagine Brad Ausmus, still with the Astros back then, is working behind the dish and the batter is Jason Bay, who was then on his way to becoming the first Pirate in their long history to win the Rookie of the Year Award.

Bay takes a mighty cut and in doing so his bat strikes the mitt of Ausmus. What would any big league umpire immediately call?

Answer on pages **110–111**

(28) Travel further back in time to 1967, the year Carl Yastrzemski won the AL Triple Crown (.326, 44 HR, 121 RBI). His Red Sox are in Chicago to take on the White Sox and he has just singled. The number four hitter in the lineup, Tony Conigliaro, steps into the batter's box and promptly hits a sharp ground ball which strikes Yaz on his right heel. While he tried to avoid contact with the ball, he was unable to do so. What's the call on this play?

Answer on page **111**

(29) Imagine Dizzy Dean is on the hill for the St. Louis Cardinals' "Gashouse Gang." He takes to the mound in the first inning with an undershirt

that has white sleeves. The home plate umpire says, "You gotta go back to the clubhouse and take that off. The white coloring can be confused with the baseball—that's a distraction." Dean complies but comes out with a blue undershirt, this one with a long sleeve on his pitching arm and a shorter sleeve on his left arm. Is this permissible under today's rule book?

Answer on page **111**

(30) In this imaginary case, Pittsburgh's Garrett Jones faces an 0–2 count, so he's defensive at the plate. The next pitch from strikeout artist Tim Lincecum hits the dirt several feet in front of home plate and ricochets, piercing through the strike zone. What's your call?

Answer on page **111**

(31) Same situation only this time Jones takes a rip at the bouncing ball and somehow laces it back through the box and into center field for an apparent single. Now what's the call?

Answer on page **112**

(32) Can an umpire eject people from a game other than players, coaches, and managers? Could he, for example, kick a fan out of the ballpark?

Answer on pages **112–113**

(33) The next scenario isn't all that tricky, but the play that leads to the question is very rare, one which stands among the most famous trick plays ever executed.

During the 1972 World Series the Oakland A's found themselves in a situation where issuing an intentional walk to Cincinnati's powerful catcher Johnny Bench made sense. So the A's went through the all the motions as if giving up a strategic walk was their true intention, including having their catcher stand up and motion to indicate he wanted his pitcher to throw a wide one. Then, startlingly, at the last second the Oakland pitcher shot the ball over the plate for a called strike three, blowing it by the relaxed, baffled Bench. Tricky, yes, but was it above board? Once the A's indicated an intentional pass and the catcher stood up, do the rules allow for such a deceitful ploy?

Answer on pages **113–114**

(34) Picture knuckleball artist Hoyt Wilhelm as he prepares to take to the mound. Because his specialty pitch is so elusive, so frustratingly difficult for catchers to handle, his receiver, Clint Courtney in this case, comes out of the dugout with an oversized catcher's mitt, one that dwarfs the normal mitt most catchers use. Is this legal?

Answer on pages **114–116**

(35) Here's a play much like one you had earlier in which a ball struck Jose Canseco on his head and then bounced into the stands. In 1977, the

Montreal Expos took on the Dodgers and Warren Cromartie smacked a deep drive to center where Rick Monday patrolled. The ball hit off the outfield wall, rebounded, struck Monday on his forehead, then flew into the stands. Should this be ruled a double or a home run?

Answer on page **116**

(36) Next, an unusual sartorial item. Houston was playing in Wrigley Field on July 28, 2009, when Cubs outfielder Kosuke Fukudome hit a low fastball into the dirt in front of home plate causing the ball to take one brisk hop then go directly into the jersey of pitcher Jeff Fulchino. The ball went through a gap between two buttons of the shirt and Fulchino had to fumble around to retrieve it. Now, once it entered his uniform was the ball dead or alive?

Answer on page **116**

(37) Let's say Ron Hunt is at the plate and a pitch tails inside on him. It barely nicks his uniform shirt but does not touch his body. Does this count as the batter being hit by a pitch or not?

Answer on pages **116–118**

(38) A few related issues: What if Hunt was hit by a pitch that was in the strike zone or by a pitch which he was swinging at—do such circumstances change anything? What if the ball was thrown so

wildly it hit the grass or dirt in front of home plate then kicked up and hit Hunt—would that qualify him for a free pass to first base?

Answer on pages **118–119**

(39) Andy Jarvis, manager of the North Coast Knights of the Prospect League (made of up college players with pro ball potential), recalled seeing a play in which all three base runners tagged up on a deep fly ball and successfully advanced one base. However, at the time of the sacrifice fly there was already one man out and the catch resulted in out number two—then, after the play, the defense appealed that the runner off first base had left early and should be the inning's third out. The umpire at first agreed, which then triggered an argument concerning the run which had scored from third on the sac fly. Does the run count or not?

Answer on pages **119–122**

(40) A wicked line drive off the bat of Arizona's Rusty Ryal drilled Los Angeles Dodgers starting pitcher Hiroki Kuroda directly on the right side of his head during a game on August 15, 2009. He collapsed on the mound, holding his head and had to be carted off the diamond. The impact was so forceful the ball ricocheted off his head, traveled all the way to a spot near the D-backs on-deck circle, then hopped into the stands.

After Kuroda departed the contest, the umpires, mirroring the show business credo that the show must go on, were required to resume play. First, though, what ruling did they make here on the Ryal hit?

Answer on pages **122–123**

(41) In his rookie season Terry Mulholland was on the mound for the San Francisco Giants on September 3, 1986. He was facing the New York Mets in the third inning when he deftly stabbed a hot grounder off the bat of Keith Hernandez.

However, when he tried to dislodge the ball from his glove he discovered he couldn't do so, at least not in time to retire the batter at first. So, thinking just as nimbly as he had fielded his position, he took a few steps toward first and lobbed his glove, ball still entrenched in the webbing, to the first baseman Bob Brenly. Did the umpire call the runner safe or out on this unusual play?

Answer on page **123**

(42) Imagine Kansas City Royals first baseman Billy Butler is at the plate. He hits a dribbler, or perhaps he lays a bunt down the third base line but somehow, in his effort to get out of the box quickly, he and the home plate umpire get tangled up (unlikely, but stick with this one). Thrown out at first by a mere step, Butler contends he would have beat the rap had it not been for the ump slowing him down. Do you award him first base on umpire's interference, do the play over, or let the out call stand?

Answer on pages **123–124**

43 Collegiate umpire Doug Nauer related an odd play he saw in 2009. "With a man on first base, a batter hit a can of corn, an easy fly ball to right field. It looked like the guy was going to make an easy catch; the batter-runner was running real hard. Well, the runner at first going to second started trotting back towards first. The right fielder drops the ball. Now the batter-runner passes the runner from first base. The runner from first base then runs to second. The guy catches the ball at second base and steps on the base." The defender at second wants the force out on the lead runner. Do you give it to him or not? What determines your decision?

Answer on page **124**

44 Umpire Sal Giacomantonio spoke of a peculiar play he once saw: "There's a runner at first base, a left-handed batter is up to bat, and the pitch comes in and the catcher tries to throw and pick off the runner at first base. He catches it. Now, when he throws it, it actually hits the batter's bat as he's standing in the box and goes out of play." What penalty is imposed here?

Answer on pages **124–125**

(45) Giacomantonio presented yet another scenario. "There's a runner at first base and there's a fly ball to right field. The guy makes a great catch and the runner realizes this and goes back to first. Now, the right fielder throws to first to try to double him off, but he overthrows and the ball goes in the stands." Straighten out this situation.

Answer on page **125**

(46) Let's say the Dodgers are playing the Giants in San Francisco. Late in this lengthy afternoon game darkness starts to set in, but not enough to have the lights turned on just yet. When the Giants come to the plate their manager, Bruce Bochy, contends it's now too dark to see well and that it is time to fire up the lights.

Is this fair or would an umpire rule that since the Dodgers played under less-than-perfect conditions, the Giants would have to do likewise for half an inning? Should he hold off on allowing the lights to come on until the top of the next inning?

Answer on page **125**

CARLOS BELTRAN

ANSWERS

(1) The correct call here is simple: McCarver is out for passing a teammate. Since he did reach first base before his rule violation, he was credited with a single instead of a home run and only one run driven in. His mental error cost him and his team one run—McCarver was penalized, but the three runners aboard were entitled to score on the "homer." His faux pas also caused him mortification and a lot of grief as teammates teased him about his blunder. However, in the long run it didn't matter as the Phillies, behind their ace, Steve Carlton, prevailed 10–5.

Years later, in the fifth game of the 1999 NLCS, Robin Ventura did something along a similar vein (losing a homer), but without such negative results—except, that is, to his stats. With the bases juiced in the last of the fifteenth inning in a 3–3 tie, Ventura scalded a pitch for a walk off grand slam against the Atlanta Braves. The only problem here was he took the term "walk off" a bit too literally and, after touching first base, he gave up on rounding the bases in order to celebrate his smash.

In a sense, he *couldn't* have completed his round trip of the bases, as he was virtually mugged by Todd Pratt, the runner off first when Ventura connected, a runner who was wise enough to touch second base before triggering the celebration by sprinting over to and hoisting Ventura in the air. Soon more teammates swarmed all over the hero whose slam, which was actually turned into a single, permitted Roger Cedeno to score the game-winning run from third. However, Ventura's failure to touch 'em all denied him the first-ever walk off "granny" in post-season history.

(2) Sometimes a call is made not simply according to the rule book, but based on how an umpire *saw the play*. In this instance, despite evidence of televised replays, the umpires, after huddling to review the initial call by Rich Garcia, who was working the right field line that day, believed they had seen no interference on the part of the young fan.

Now, had they ruled that the young boy had prevented Tarasco, who had just come in the game as a defensive replacement for Bobby Bonilla, from making the catch, they would have ruled Jeter out. As it was, Jeter, then a rookie batting in the number-nine slot, had his first ever post-season homer and the Yanks went on to win the game in the eleventh inning when Bernie Williams hit a legitimate homer and New York breezed to win the pennant in five games. Garcia later, upon seeing replays, admitted he had missed the call, but it was too late for the lamenting Orioles.

In a 2009 interview, Tarasco said of the play, "People ask me if that ball should have been a ground-rule double, but no, that ball was caught. One hundred percent I was going to catch it."

(3) There is no fan interference. That infraction cannot, by rule, be called when the ball is in (or more precisely, above) the stands. In other words, if the ball is above the field of play, the fielder and not the fan has the right to catch it and must not be interfered with. However, as in our case, once the ball's path takes it into the stands, a fan is permitted to touch it. Bartman, a Cubs fan, should have backed off and made room for Alou to make his catch (and, given more time to think rather than merely react, he might have). So, while what he did was "legal," by preventing Alou from recording a vital out, he brought down the animus of millions of Cubs fans.

Chicago sportswriter and editor of *Baseball Digest*, John Kuenster, covering the game, saw the play otherwise. "In my mind, there was fan interference. I was at an angle, looking straight down the line there and Bartman's hands were over the line [jutting into the playing area] and that's why Alou got so angry—he was going to catch that ball, but the left field umpire was running at an angle where he couldn't tell so he didn't call fan interference."

Kuenster said he didn't blame the fan for doing what comes naturally, reaching out for a souvenir. He recalled Bartman getting abused unmercifully, but said, "I blame the umpire—he didn't call it." That, said Kuenster, may have changed Cubs history. If Alou caught the ball or got an out call on the interference, "maybe the Cubs would've won that game, [and] they're in the World Series." They were, in fact, just five outs shy of clinching the game and advancing to the Series before the notorious play took place—which, incidentally, involved other fans reaching for the ball and impeding Alou, not just Bartman.

One thing is certain—moments after Bartman impeded Alou, Prior began to struggle. Here's how it all unraveled: First, he walked Castillo, and then he uncorked a wild pitch. Next came a line drive single to left by Ivan Rodriguez to score Pierre and send Castillo darting into third. Miguel Cabrera hit a grounder for what should have been the second out of the inning but shortstop Alex Gonzalez committed a costly error, allowing the Marlins to load the bases.

Then the floodgates opened. Derrek Lee sent a line drive double screaming into left field to drive home two, ending the night for Prior. Kyle Farnsworth came into the contest, issued an intentional base on balls to Mike Lowell, a sac fly to Jeff Conine to give Florida the lead, another intentional free pass (this one to Todd Hollandsworth), and then surrendered a three-run line drive double to Mike Mordecai, once more to the busy Alou in left field.

At that point Mike Remlinger entered the game to face Pierre, who singled for the eighth run of the nightmarish inning. Finally, Castillo, the twelfth batter of the inning, ended things by popping out. The damage was done, though, and Florida, on the ninety-fifth anniversary of the last time the Cubs had won the World Championship, held the lead, winning by an 8–3 score to send the NLCS to a seventh game.

In that contest the Cubs, as doomed as perennial loser Charlie Brown, had star pitcher Kerry Wood as their starter, yet gave up a 5–3 lead in the fifth inning and ultimately fell to the eventual World Series champs by a score of 9–6.

(4) Not exactly. Richards didn't have to manipulate the rule book, per se; he simply didn't *remove* his pitcher from the game—if he had, the pitcher is gone for good (unlike some amateur levels of baseball, the major leagues have a no re-entry rule). What Richards did was ingenious and is a move other managers have since done from time to time. He had Pierce replace his starting first baseman, but only for the one out his relief pitcher, Harry Dorish, managed to record. Then, the cagey manager simply moved Pierce from his spot at first, reinserted him now as a "reliever," replacing Dorish. Of course he did lose his starting first baseman, but was willing to do so in this situation. It should be noted that another version of this strategy states Richards once brought in Pierce to face fellow lefty Ted Williams, moved Dorish, normally a reliever but the starter that day, to third, then returned him to the mound after Pierce had retired the "Splendid Splinter."

Longtime coach Johnny Goryl said he saw managers employ this tactic when Sam McDowell and Kent Tekulve were pitching but added, "Back in those days we only had eight- or nine-man pitching staffs; ten was the most clubs carried. Today we've got thirteen-man staffs so you don't see this [gimmick used] much more now."

5 The Canseco play was ruled a (painful) home run by both the umpire and the official scorer who could have ruled it a rare four-base error.

"In my life I've never seen anything like that," said Indians General Manager John Hart with a chuckle, "I was stunned. I've seen balls hit outfielders on the head before, but not one that bounced over the fence." Writers then asked Texas infielder Julio Franco if he had ever seen such a play. "Yeah," he responded, "in a cartoon."

Toronto's Alex Rios was involved in a similar strange play on August 31, 2006, when Boston's Alex Cora lifted a fly ball to the outfield. Rios reached the ball after a long run, only to have it bounce in and out of his glove. He then tried to capture the ball in his bare hand but instead tapped it into the right field stands in Fenway Park. Rios later said he should have caught the ball which some felt he had overrun slightly. Nevertheless, the official scorer awarded Cora a home run.

6 If McCray had made a grab of the ball prior to his running through the fence, it would have held up as a legal catch for an amazing out.

As a side note, on August 12, 2006, the Portland team honored McCray with a "Rodney McCray Bobblefence [not bobble*head*] Night." He threw out the first pitch of the game and was further immortalized when the club renamed the right-center field area of the stadium (which then bore the name PGE Park) as "McCray's Alley." According to Wikipedia, McCray commented, "I just wish I had run through something like a Coca-Cola sign so I could have gotten endorsements. Instead, I ran through a local sign, 'Flav-R-Pac Meats.'" He stated he never felt the warning track and thus never slowed down. While he was shaken up on the play, the injuries he sustained were not serious. The television program *The Best Damn Sports Show Period* named the McCray play the number-one moment on their list of the "Top 50 Devastating Hits" in the history of sports.

McCray, who winced the first time he saw the play on video, now says he never tires of talking about his play and he compared himself to being "like the skier who epitomizes the 'agony of defeat'—I'm the guy who crashed through the wall."

So, once more, had he have made the catch, Hale would have been out and McCray's play would not have been declared a homer nor a ground-rule double. By the way, even though many fans and even announcers get this wrong, it is *not* a ground rule double when, for example, a ball hits somewhere in fair territory on the playing surface then bounds over the outfield wall. (This used to happen a slew of times when so many of the major league parks' outfield surface consisted of very springy and resilient artificial turf, such as the original fake stuff known as Astroturf.) This most certainly is a *book* rule as it comes directly from the official rule book and applies to *all* ballparks; it is *not* a rule that pertains only to the park, i.e., the "grounds," where a given team plays their home games.

For example, a ball hitting a speaker at, Tropicana Field, indoor home of the Tampa Bay Rays, is subject to the local rule—again, the rule is indigenous to *that park*. Another domed facility may well have different rules about the quirks of its ballpark. For instance, any ball striking a speaker in Seattle's original big league ballpark, the Kingdome, was live. Further, that facility used to have fourteen loudspeakers as well as fifty-nine wires and seventy-five streamers above the diamond which could come into play. Several foul balls hit speakers and were grabbed by the defense for outs; and once the powerful six-foot, six-inch Dave Kingman teed off on a ball which was easily headed over the wall, only to see it bounce off a speaker and be caught for an out.

In the Metrodome in Minneapolis Randy Bush of the Twins once hit a ball that soared all the way up to the roof, hit it then deflected to Toronto catcher Buck Martinez for an unusual foul out. Finally, on May 4, 1984, in that same ballpark Kingman launched a ball that incredibly sailed through a hole in the roof and never came back down—it left the park but the umpires gave him a double.

(7) Dietz does not get to take a leisurely walk to first base. While Dietz was hit by the pitch, Harry Wendelstedt, in just his second year umping in the majors, made a gutsy and perfectly correct call. He decided that Dietz, in making no effort to avoid being struck, gave up his right to first base. Because the pitch was inside, it was called ball

three and Drysdale eventually induced Dietz to fly out to shallow left field, keeping his remarkable streak intact. Sucking it up even more, Drysdale then got out of his jam by retiring two pinch hitters—Ty Cline hit into a first-to-home force play, Wes Parker to Jeff Torborg, and Jack Hiatt popped up to Parker. In his next start on June 4, he lowered his ERA to 1.31, knocking off the Pittsburgh Pirates and Jim Bunning, yet another future Hall of Fame pitcher, 5–0. The shutout string eventually ran just one out shy of fifty-nine consecutive scoreless innings and covered a record six straight shutouts.

Drysdale's skein ended after opening his June 8 start with four and two-thirds scoreless innings before surrendering a sacrifice fly. His record was one that would hold up for almost exactly twenty years until 1988, when a fellow Dodger great, Orel Hershiser, officially went him one out better, working fifty-nine straight shutout innings (wrapping the record up on his last start of September 28) before his skein ended in the first inning of Opening Day of the following season. His streak, then, stayed locked in at fifty-nine innings.

It's difficult to believe, but on the 1968 season, Drysdale's penultimate year, despite an ERA of 2.15 and his total of eight shutouts, his record was just two games over .500 at 14–12. Not to diminish what he accomplished, but that season was known as the "Year of the Pitcher" with many fantastic pitching achievements being turned in—it was almost the pitchers' version of the sluggers'"Steroid Era" in that regard. For example, Detroit's Denny McLain won a staggering thirty-one contests, Bob Gibson posted an unfathomable ERA of 1.12, still among the lowest ever (third-best in the modern era), and Luis Tiant of the Red Sox led all AL pitchers with his 1.60 ERA, making him one of five men in the league with an ERA under 2.00. In fact, the average ERA for all of major league baseball was just a shade under 3.00, and Drysdale's mark ranked only sixth in the NL.

By the way, some players have been way too blatant in their efforts to reach first base via duplicity. Umpire Ryan Burich says he once worked an amateur game in which a batter not only made no effort to avoid being hit by a pitch, "He just threw his elbow right out at the pitch." There was no way he was going to be awarded first base on that one.

(8) It was a judgment call on Burkhart's part and the out stood. However, one source said Carbo should have been safe because he was never tagged properly and, when he went over to argue the call with Burkhart, he accidentally did step on home plate.

When asked what he thought about the chaotic play, Casey Stengel said, "It was a dead heat: Carbo missed the plate, Hendricks missed the tag, and Burkhart missed the call." Burkhart ruminated, "That was quite a play ... and I was on my behind."

(9) To play it safe and to avoid any possible confusion, runners should turn to their right to return to first base after overrunning it—no

need to have an umpire misconstrue your intentions and call you out. Still, the runner here made no real effort to bolt for second and he should be called safe.

In the majors, the only time you might see a runner called out on a play like this occurs when he overruns first, spots a defensive misplay such as the ball getting away from the first baseman, then, initially believing he can make it to second, he makes a clear move towards second, reconsiders, and is tagged out as he scrambles back toward first base.

(10) The umpires measured the batter's box and Martin was correct—the box was seven feet long, not the prescribed six feet. Seattle manager Maury Wills, in a case of gamesmanship (or cheating), had instructed his groundskeeper to make the box longer so his batters, such as Paciorek, could set themselves up deeper than normal while facing Oakland's Rick Langford. Ultimately the league, not the umpires, punished Wills, dishing out a two-game suspension.

(11) Most fans realize the ball was fair, but Goetz also had to know that the ball was also still live because, by rule, the coach is considered to be, in effect, "part of the field." Had it ricocheted further away, say into the foul grounds out by left field, the speedy LeFlore might have risked stretching his hit. As it was, he settled for a strange single. Actually, in this case, the announcers said they believed that the ball would have

bounced off the bag and into the dugout had it not struck the coach. Had that been so, a different ruling would have come into play.

Two incidental items: 1) Fidrych did go on to win the game and from there racked up eleven more wins to end the year at 19–9 with a sterling 2.34 ERA, stats easily good enough to earn him the Rookie of the Year Award. However, injuries led to his early baseball demise; he would go a mere 10–10 over the rest of his truncated career; 2) Bob Prince said the play in question rather reminded him of the time he saw Pittsburgh's Dick Stuart hit a ball which bounded over a base, struck an object, and eventually came to rest inside a rolled up tarpaulin at Wrigley Field. The call there? Well, because there was, at the time, no ground rule to cover such an unlikely event, Prince stated Stuart picked up a cheap inside-the-park home run on the play.

(12) Amateur umpire Pete Carbonaro explained, "It's a no call. You stand there." In other words, there is no signal given by the ump. Usually, Carbonaro said, the runner simply strolls back to and stands on the base. "That's when you make the call. Safe."

(13) By rule, Miller's movement made him guilty of a balk. The gust of wind was an act of God, and Miller certainly wasn't trying to deceive a runner, but it's a balk, nonetheless.

Miller, however, didn't see it that way. "They didn't call it right away. I delivered the pitch to the plate and Rocky Colavito was the hitter—he swung at it and missed and *then* the umpire decides he's going to call a balk on me. In an All-Star Game they have umpires everywhere. Six umpires and not one of them called a balk. The home plate umpire, who didn't even see it, came out and [finally] called the balk. If he'd have seen me balk, he would have called it immediately, so I don't know what happened."

(14) Jackson interfered with the throw and the correct call should have been that he was out and so was Piniella—double play and end of inning. Of course, had there been no outs, the double play would still stand, the ball would have been declared dead, and no other runner(s) could advance. However, the umpires that day didn't see it that way and ruled Jackson had done nothing improper.

Sal Giacomantonio said, "The call that was made was incorrect, but it's a judgment call. The replays showed Reggie did have some intent in his [swinging] his hip out there to draw contact. What happens is sometimes [such a play] surprises you—you would never expect it to happen. Unfortunately, we're supposed to make quick decisions, especially back in that era. Umpires very rarely reversed calls; now they do it more frequently in order to get it right, but back in the day, you live and die with the call. In that situation I'm sure that umpire, when he went home and saw the replays, probably didn't sleep very well."

(15) Picture this: A manager brings in a reliever, a move which could then be countered by the offense sending up a new pinch hitter only to have the defensive team counter by having yet another reliever being trotted out of the bullpen. This back-and-forth maneuvering could go on all day if it weren't for the rule which states that once a new pitcher enters a game he must face and dispose of at least one batter by either getting him out or by having him reach base. Thus, in our question Leyland is committed to the first reliever he called into the game.

Interestingly, a relief pitcher once dispatched the first hitter he faced (and more) doing so in a very unusual way. As a matter of fact, he not only got credit for working a full inning by facing just one batter, he needed to lob but one single pitch to do so. In addition to that, he also earned the win that day by throwing just that one pitch.

On July 27, 1930, Ken Ash of the Cincinnati Reds came into a ball game in relief of Larry Benton. He induced Chicago's Charlie Grimm to hit into a triple play on his very first pitch. Before he could take to the mound again, Ash was lifted for a pinch hitter. Furthermore, when the Reds rallied and took the lead for good that same inning, Ash was given credit for the victory. He managed to chalk up one of the quickest wins in baseball history, a very easy, economical one at that.

(16) Jordan was awarded one extra base on Leibrandt's mental lapse.

(17) Seemingly everything Perry did was illegal by the end of his career, so by that time this is one of those rule infractions.

New rules sometimes had to be created to combat his tactics. For example, pitchers used to be permitted to freely put their fingers up to their mouth, any time, anywhere, but that was revised so a pitcher could lick his pitching hand, but he had to immediately wipe his hands off. The coy Perry reportedly wiped his fingers, but not the ones he had wet; he could, and would, still throw his illegal pitch. So now the rule states that unless umpires give permission to both pitchers to put their hand to their mouth—this happens usually on very cold days when the umps permit the pitchers to blow on their meat hand—a pitcher may only do this action if they are entirely off the mound.

As a side note, late in his career when Perry was once more looking for any edge, he concocted another distraction. Prior to a pitch he would take the resin bag and shake it around until a ton of the powdery substance was on his pitching hand. The result was the next pitch came out of his hand amid a puff of smoke, a tactic that was also banned later. By 2007, a rule states that any pitcher who taints a ball shall be ejected from the game.

Perry often denied loading up a spitball saying, "That's the pitch they *thought* I threw—I never did." However, once in a moment of whimsy and candor, he admitted, "I'd always have [grease] in at least two places, in case the umpires would ask me to wipe off one. I never wanted to be caught out there without anything." Then he added ironically, "It wouldn't be professional." Perry even threw an illegal pitch in an old timer's game to Art Kusnyer, who muttered in disbelief, "He threw me a spitter!"

A winner of 314 contests, Perry was ejected from a game only once. That took place for having a foreign substance on his person and for allegedly using his spitball in a game against the Red Sox on August 23, 1982 (he also wound up being stung with a ten-day suspension as well). Perry joked about how he enjoyed getting into opponents' heads: "I just remember putting grease on my hand and shaking hands with the opponents the day before I pitched. I wanted them to think about it."

He sometimes contended he was throwing an early version of a split-finger fastball, calling his pitch a Cuban forkball. When asked if it took him long to learn the pitch, he laughed, "Not when you're 1–6," referring to the fact that when he first mastered the forkball, a pitch he came to throw as "a good off-speed pitch," he was young and desperate, straddled with a losing record and well aware that if he didn't come up with an out pitch, it was back to the minors or to oblivion for him.

Another side note: Don Sutton was also suspected of doctoring a baseball now and again. "I ought to get a Black and Decker commercial out of it," he once said about his alleged scuffing of baseballs. One day umpire Jim Evans was behind the plate during a Sutton start. Believing Sutton had indeed been throwing an illegal pitch, perhaps doing so by scuffing it with, say, a nail file hidden on his person, Evans made a trek out to the mound to examine the pitcher. When he asked Sutton to show him what he had in his pocket, the pitcher, with the flair of a magician, produced a card from a pocket and handed it to Evans. The card read, "You're getting warm."

(18) Younger fans may miss this question because in today's game players rub elbows behind the batting cage as freely and as easily as teenagers used to congregate and mingle at a malt shop. However, in an earlier era there was actually a rule against fraternizing with the opposition.

At one point it was fairly rigidly enforced—during pre-game activities an umpire was stationed in the stands to spy on such "trysts." If he saw opposing players becoming chummy, he would write up a report and the violators would be slapped with a small fine—$25 for breaking the rule the first time and double that for the second infraction. One imagines a modern player getting such a fine, pulling out a wad of money the size of George Costanza's wallet, peeling off a thousand-dollar bill, while sneering, "Here. When that runs out, come see me again."

Bob Friend, who pitched in the major leagues from 1951 through 1966, said he never knew of a player getting fined for breaking this rule, but the warning was clear. He also said that when players from rival teams socialized with each other it didn't look good to the fans who wanted their team to be hungry and to dislike the enemy, not pal around with them.

Retired umpire Dave Phillips told a *Sporting News* writer he didn't care for the rule due to the fact that "you would have to get confrontational with a player before the game even started." The rule, wrote Stan McNeal, "eventually phased itself out" and "by the mid-1980s, the league had stopped enforcing it."

(19) The key to this question is the phrase "before the lineup cards are turned over to the umpires." Aside from those games in which a team is making its last trip through a city—canceling such games means they may not get made up later or, if they have some bearing on the playoff picture, they will be played but with inconveniences such as rescheduling flights and hotel rooms—the home team decides if a game should start or not. Technically the rules stipulate that the manager of the home team makes this call, but in practice it's often the decision of the general manager (sometimes in conjunction with others such as the field manager). The front office and the umpires are, of course, in constant touch with others, for example the National Weather Service, to help make the "play or don't play" decision.

In August 1990, the White Sox management decided to hold off on calling a game despite the presence of a heavy, long storm. Their decision caused fans to endure a seven hour and twenty-three-minute rain delay; and after all of that, they still postponed the game. Chicago was in a pennant race and it was the last trip into town for the visiting Rangers, but it seemed very unfair to the waterlogged fans.

Once the lineup cards are turned over to the umpires, all such decisions belong to them (specifically the crew chief) with two exceptions: the second game of doubleheaders and cases when the commissioner's office decides to step in to make the call—in reality no single party makes the decision. Big league umpire Fieldin Culbreth confirmed that such high-level decisions typically take place involving games late in the season, when calling off contests can be tricky due to scheduling conflicts, thus causing the completion of games which may have a bearing on postseason play to become more crucial. "Down the stretch when the season's just about over and there are no dates to reschedule and there's very little time to get these games played, we just bring one more set of minds into it, which is the commissioner's office, and we talk about the logistics of how we're going to do this. It's just more people getting involved in the process." And all those people must consider one key element, said Culbreth: "If we cancel the game, what are we going to be able to do to make it up?"

Culbreth elaborated further, "No matter what the rule is, no umpire makes that decision [to call a game off] without a whole lot of conversation both managers, the general managers, and field personnel. We don't just go out there, get the lineup cards, then in the fifth inning when it starts raining just decide to go home. It's raining too hard; we're going home.

"There's a whole lot of things that come into play. First of all, there are rules that say you have to wait a certain amount of time. Behind the scenes, the crew chief is speaking with multiple weathermen . . . and just kind of getting the impression of what people want to do, and he's weighing all those options and then he's trying to put two and two together and come up with a decision. You're just taking everybody's point of view and weighing it into the decision that you ultimately have to make."

Umpires will consult with the grounds crew as well. "We're asking, 'How wet is the field already? How do you think it's going to hold up if it continues to rain like this? Is it going to rain all night from what we're hearing?' We're talking about people who work on it [the field] every day—they know how much water it can take."

What also complicates decisions are factors such as if the game is in the early innings before it's become official. No team, especially a "team that can't afford a loss," wants a game in which they lead to be called. "You're also talking about revenues. Nobody's down there trying to influence our decision. It's not something you take lightly and it's not something that you go into by yourself—there are plenty of people that are in on that decision."

Incidentally, over the years there have been some bizarre reasons for games to be delayed, postponed, or cancelled. Red Hudler recalled a time in Montreal when, in an extremely rare occasion, the Expos decided to open the dome roof at old Olympic Stadium. "They [then] closed it one night and it rained. There were a couple of leaks in the roof that were so bad, they had to postpone a game. It was the first rainout ever in an indoor stadium."

That was not unlike a game that took place in Toronto on June 5, 1989, between the Blue Jays, who were unveiling their new ballpark that day, and the Milwaukee Brewers. The roof of Skydome was being shut, a procedure that normally takes in the neighborhood of twenty minutes, but it jammed before it could be entirely closed. That left a gap, wrote Philip J. Lowry, which resulted in "a waterfall to shower down directly on the batter, catcher, and umpire" and a lengthy delay.

On July 22, 2000, the Mariners game versus the Rangers was delayed by rain for nearly an hour even though the teams were playing in Seattle's domed ballpark, Safeco Field. It seems the $517.6-million roof wouldn't close due to a computer problem that took twenty minutes to solve.

Another time fog was the cause of a delay in yet another domed stadium. The Skydome roof had been opened at the start of the contest versus the Braves before fog began rolling in. It became so thick umpire Greg Kosc said he could no longer follow the flight of an Andruw Jones's fly ball. He ordered the roof shut and the game then recommenced.

Games have also been known to be interrupted by high winds, swarms of bees or gnats, and power outages. Once in Montreal the start of a game was held up when the grounds crew had to corral some elusive circus seals from a pre-game promotion.

By the way, the rule book covers when to close an opened roof. Here's one simple example: If a contest starts with the roof open, it may only be ordered to be shut if conditions such as "impending rain" may "affect play or spectator comfort." If the home team feels that is the case, they are to discuss their concerns with the umpire crew chief, who then notifies the visiting team. If they don't mind, then the order is given to close the roof. However, if they object, wary that "a competitive imbalance will arise," the crew chief must make a ruling. Also, though few fans realize it, a rule states that a roof is only permitted to be moved once during a ball game. If, for instance, the roof was closed due to a threat of a rainstorm, it may not be reopened during that contest.

(20) Hoak has no right to contend the batter should be awarded a single. He caused the ball to make contact with him—he's out on his interference but, and here's the surprising part, the batter did reach first base and Gilliam was permitted to advance to second. Hoak did thwart a double play, but only because at the time, wrote Carl Erskine in his *Tales from the Dodgers Dugout*, there was no rule covering such an infraction. Now, of course, he'd be out and so would the batter; any other runner(s) could not move up on the play.

(21) This is yet another situation which wasn't covered by the rule book at the time. Stanky, like Hoak, was responsible for a change being made to the rules. As a post script to the play, Seminick, like a deadly free-throw artist ignoring fans waving their arms behind the basket, got his job done, reaching first base. Soon after, a grounder was hit and Stanky, covering second for the force play, "was taken out of action by a crunching football block" by the bent-on-payback Seminick, a man Richie Ashburn described as one you never wanted to rile up.

(22) Bragan, ninety-one years-old when he discussed this play in an April 2009 interview, recalled what happened decades ago, back on August 18, 1965, at old Sportsman's Park in St. Louis. "Chris Pelekoudas, the plate umpire, called [Aaron] out when he hit the ball. Hank circled the bases and he came home and, [when Aaron discovered his homer was disallowed] he threw Aaron out of the game and of course I went with him." The rule which Pelekoudas enforced does state that if a batter has one foot entirely out of the box, not touching even an iota of chalk from the batter's box, he is to be called out. Bragan, disagreeing with the call, still points out Aaron "would have had another home run," which would have put his final total at 756 over his marvelous twenty-three seasons.

Baseball Digest quoted Simmons as saying, "Aaron was anticipating a slow curve. He moved up in the batter's box to meet the curve before it broke." According to this account, "He hit the ball on the right field roof and took a few steps toward first before Pelekoudas called him out."

Aaron's recollections of the odd play were similar to those of Bragan and Simmons. Aaron stated, "It was a changeup and I probably stepped out of the batter's box. My foot probably was out, and I don't know if I was anxious—Curt Simmons was one of the toughest pitchers for me to hit. As a young hitter I had never really understood how to step back and wait and hit the ball, you know. Later on I did a pretty good job of it, but that one particular year I just didn't have all of my hitting ability there."

It should also be noted that the batter is out even if the ball he hit lands foul—and that counts a foul tip, too. The ball is to be declared dead and if there are any runners on base, they are frozen at the base they held when the pitch was made.

23 Although warnings are typically issued to rein in pitchers bent on payback, Davidson was certainly permitted to kick a pitcher out of a game in such a situation.

   The last time a pitcher had been sent to the showers so quickly had been Pittsburgh's Zack Duke in 2005, but in his case he departed after being struck by a wicked line drive which broke his thumb.

24 Wegner made the correct call based on what he saw. However, the home plate ump reversed his call when informed of the obstruction. Third base umpire Rob Drake informed Wegner of his call and Wegner then reversed his decision. Drake felt, contact or not, Sizemore had been slowed down by the Reds' third baseman, and that constituted obstruction.

25 Although, by the very definition of the infield fly rule, the batter is always automatically out in such situations, the runners off first and second were free to advance at their own risk. Because they both tried to move up a base and failed, the end result was a zany triple play.

26 While placing Hershiser in the starting lineup as a third baseman was certainly strange, there was a logical reason behind this Dodgers move. With Los Angeles hitting first, Manager Tommy Lasorda never had Hershiser even pop his head out of the dugout. Instead, when it was his turn to bat, Dave Hansen came off the bench to pinch hit.

The move was merely a ploy to give Hansen, who stayed in the game after hitting, one official pinch at bat. He was in the process of trying to break the record for the most pinch hits in a season by a Dodger. The move is perfectly legal, though rare.

(27) The correct call is catcher's interference, causing Bay to be awarded first base—providing he didn't hit the ball and, say, hit an extra base hit. In that case the umpire wouldn't penalize Bay but would allow his hit to stand. The offense may choose to accept what happened on the play after contact with the mitt took place and ignore the penalty. If the batter hit, say, a sacrifice fly to drive home a key run, the offense may choose to take the play, giving up the out in exchange for a run scored.

In order for catcher's interference to be called (which results in an error being charged on the catcher), the mitt must make contact with the bat before the completion of the hitter's swing. Also, if the hitter is able to reach first base regardless of the contact with the catcher's mitt *and* if all runners on base advanced one notch safely, then the interference call is ignored.

According to the Baseball Analysts Web site, Yankee outfielder Roberto Kelly got first base a record eight times on this play in 1992. It seems fitting that the man who reached first base on hits more than any player ever, Pete Rose, managed to finagle his way to first on catcher's interference more times (twenty-nine) than any other ballplayer.

Five times in baseball history a player has reached first base on the play twice in a game and two of these hitters were catchers themselves: Bob Stinson of the 1977 Mariners and Pat Corrales as a member of the Reds in 1965. In fact, Corrales did it two times that year, on August 15 and again on September 29.

(28) Like catcher's interference, this is one of the oddest and most obscure ways of reaching first base safely because the ruling on the play is this: The base runner, in this instance Yaz, is automatically out even though he touched the ball accidentally, and the batter, Tony Conigliaro, is credited with a base hit.

There are, it should be noted, exceptions to this rule. The runner must be touched by the ball is fair territory and that contact must occur before the ball has either touched a fielder or, for example, when the infield is drawn in, the ball has passed a fielder.

(29) No. The sleeves of the undershirt not only can't be white, they also must be of equal length.

(30) Once the ball hit the turf before it crossed the plate in this scenario it's a ball.

111

(31) Now things are different. Again, if Jones had laid off the pitch it would be called a ball, but he chose to swing at the ball and it is certainly his right to do so. Once he swings, however, whatever happens, happens. Herb Score once said that while he couldn't remember the hitter's name, a long time ago when Score bounced a pitch up to the plate the batter swung, connected, and drove it out of the park for a most peculiar home run.

(32) Umpires have full authority to run a game and, by extension, to "run" anyone from the game.

Former ump "Duke" Rash recalled one such instance. "One time my partner, Bruce Froemming, threw some fellows out from the press box because they referred to us on the P.A. system as the 'Three Blind Mice.' He called the security guy down and he says, 'I want them removed from the press box,' and that was it."

In June 2009 wire service reports told of an ump who, using his near-dictatorial power, "emptied the stands at a high school game in West Burlington, Iowa, ejecting the entire crowd of more than 100 fans for being unruly." He indicated he had no difficulties with the players during the contest between Winfield-Mount Union and West Burlington, just the adults in the stands.

During his playing days Terry Francona was once chased from a game just moments after he had drawn an intentional walk. With bad blood already existing between him and home plate ump Ken Kaiser,

Francona fumed when Kaiser muttered, "Can you believe they're intentionally walking *you*?" Having been insulted, Francona snapped, and accused the umpire of not hustling on a play earlier in that series. Then, seconds later, after ball four had been served up, Kaiser gave him the thumb.

Charlie Williams once ejected a manager before a game even began. The manager brought a videotape of a disputed call from the previous day's game for Williams to view. Williams must have felt his authority was being questioned and booted the manager on the spot.

Umpires even have to power to make a ruling when something that takes place in a game is not covered anywhere in the rule book. Umpires are, metaphorically, the Moe Howard of the baseball world, always getting the final say. In short, their power is almost limitless.

(33) There was nothing to stop the A's from fooling Bench, whose job it was to be alert. In 1995, the Cleveland tandem of catcher Tony Pena and pitcher Dennis Martinez recreated that deception, pulling it off on the first of two occasions. The first time they pulled the trick on California's Chili Davis with a full count and a runner on third.

Pena came out of his crouch and signaled for an intentional walk. Just as Bench had done, Davis relaxed. Martinez slipped the third strike by Davis who later commented, "I got suckered. I've never seen it before and I'll never see it again."

Just one year later, on July 30, 1996, Pena initiated the play again with Toronto's John Olerud as the victim. Martinez and Pena again worked their con game perfectly, this time on a two-out, 3–2 delivery.

(34) There are limits as to the size of gloves and mitts worn by big leaguers, but the oversized one used by the catcher in our question was within the limits. The current rule has since shrunk the legal circumference of catcher's mitts down to thirty-eight inches—the first oversized mitt checked in at a whopping forty-five inches in circumference. Today's mitts also have other restrictions—for example, they may not be "more than fifteen and one-half inches from top to bottom," according to rule 1.12.

Baltimore manager Paul Richards, a former big league catcher, was the innovator of the first oversized mitt, the one used to accommodate Oriole pitcher Hoyt Wilhelm, possessor of one of the game's greatest knucklers ever and the first reliever ever to be honored by Hall of Fame induction (in 1985).

The unveiling of Richards's strange mitt took place on May 27, 1960, when Courtney went behind the plate with it, attempting to corral Wilhelm's elusive pitch. One year earlier Orioles' catchers had been guilty of a record-setting forty-nine passed balls, thirty-eight of which came when Wilhelm was on the hill.

Sportswriter Tom Meany once observed, "Hoyt always had more trouble with his own catchers than he did with opposing batters." Meanwhile, former catcher Hal Smith said he didn't like the oversized mitt. "I didn't want to use it. I said, 'I can catch better without it.'" However, to this day such mitts are used by big leaguer catchers who still give thanks to Richards for his contribution to the men who don the tools of ignorance.

Wilhelm, incidentally, has been linked to several interesting trivia items over the years. First of all, although he didn't make it to the majors until he was twenty-eight years old, he came out swinging, hitting a home run in his first big league game at bat. While he stuck around for twenty-one years (working his final big league game just sixteen days short of his fiftieth birthday) and appeared in a then-record 1,070 games, he never again hit one out. Second, over his career he only started fifty-two games, yet in the only year he started more than eleven times (1959 when he was the starter in twenty-seven contests) he led his league in ERA. Remarkably, he had also led the league in that department once while working exclusively out of the bullpen—in 1952, his rookie season. That year he toiled in $159\frac{1}{3}$ innings, a total not only good enough to qualify him for league leadership, but one that dwarfs the totals of today's bullpen inhabitants.

Catcher's mitts and knuckleballers aside, the basic limitations for first basemen's mitts is they cannot be longer than twelve inches from the top to the bottom, or "more than eight inches wide across the palm." The size limit for all other fielders is, again without getting into all the nuances, twelve inches from the heel of the glove to the tip of the longest finger of the glove.

(35) Because the ball first hit off the outfield wall, it is ruled a bounding ball and cannot be declared a home run—it didn't clear the fence before striking a part of the playing field. It's a double.

(36) The ball is in play. Fukudome easily reached first base before Fulchino could fish the ball out of his jersey.

In a 1979 contest another Cubs outfielder, Larry Biittner, dove in an attempt to catch a low liner hit by Mets batter Bruce Boisclair, but came up empty. When he tried to locate the ball to throw it back in, he couldn't—the ball had vanished. Actually, it had come to rest under his cap which had come off during his stab for the ball. Boisclair rambled all the way to third, where he was thrown out on this zany play.

(37) Yes, it counts. If a pitched ball makes contact with a player or his uniform including padding, jersey, belt, helmet, and pants, he is awarded first base and the ball is dead.

Hunt was a scrappy player who strove to reach base any way he could. On tight pitches he willingly allowed the ball to hit him, making only a minimal effort to get out of the path of the pitch—just enough so an umpire wouldn't rule he wasn't entitled to first base because he made no effort to avoid contact.

He even allowed himself to get hit by a pitch in an old-timers' game not once, but twice—once by Len Barker who, though retired, was still in shape at the time of the exhibition game and threw hard that day. A teammate seeing Hunt get drilled by Barker shook his head saying, "Things never change." Hunt later commented, "When you're dumb, you're dumb," and laughed off being hit by Gaylord Perry: "Gaylord can't hurt you [by throwing his junk]." As for being hit hard by Barker, Hunt smiled, "If they throw hard, I'll take one for the team. If you can't hit them, let them hit you."

He knew how to roll with the punches, so to speak, often letting a ball hit him in places where the pain would be relatively minor. He also wore billowy shirts and baggy pants, hoping balls would graze him there. As sportswriter Furman Bisher noted, "Hunt wore a shirt big enough to accommodate Ringling Bros. …You get hit easier with a size 48 than you do a size 42." Needless to say, Hunt crowded the plate the way a glutton bellies up to a buffet bar.

One of his managers, Gene Mauch, commented, "I wouldn't say he goes to bat to get hit, but I also wouldn't say he has ever seen a pitch he'd dodge."

He was so adept at his art form he once simultaneously held the single-season record (fifty, still the modern mark and almost exactly one time hit for each three games he played in, 1971) and career record (243, now third-best in the modern era behind only Craig Biggio and Don Baylor) for the most times getting plunked by a pitch. He led his league in that department seven times, all in a row, good for yet another record. Once he led the NL when he was hit an incredible forty-one times more than the runner up. In addition, one year he led his team in that category, being hit on twenty-four occasions, when the second highest tally of the team was a mere eighth of his total.

(38) If a batter swings at a pitch which hits him or if he is hit while that part of his body, say one of his hands, is in the strike zone, the ball is dead but the pitch counts as a strike—he does not get first base.

Though it is rare, this play actually took place not too long ago, when Casey Blake was still with Cleveland. The Indians had made a trip into Boston to play the Red Sox. With two strikes on him, Blake swung at a pitch just as it hit him. As amateur umpire Ryan Burich explained, some fans felt "it was a do-over, but since he swung, it's a dead ball, strike three. No one can advance; no one can do anything else."

Incidentally, if a pitched ball hits the ground first, then the batter, even if he is in the strike zone, does get a free stroll to first.

Another pertinent point here: umpire Sal Giacomantonio observed that there is only one "do-over" in baseball. "Let's say that the umpires do not notice that there are not nine fielders. Let's say the left fielder has to go to the bathroom in between innings. The umpires and the players don't realize it. They start the inning with the left fielder not in position—he's still in the bathroom. Now the batter comes up and he hits a home run. Believe it or not, they say, 'Hey, wait a minute. We didn't have nine players on the field.' They start over from the beginning of the inning, [taking away the homer]."

Thus the offense could get punished "for a mistake that the defense did, which doesn't make sense, but that was one of those plays we covered in umpire school. That's why the umpires need to make sure that all the fielders are in fair territory and that there's the proper amount of people there." Plus, he added, even if, say, two more batters came to the plate and hit safely before the missing player situation was corrected, "You're going to go all the way back to the beginning of the inning."

(39) The runner who left first base early is, of course, out to end the inning, but the run, contrary to what most fans think, does count. As Giacomantonio clarified, "In that situation it's actually a time play. It doesn't matter that the guy left early because the run crossed the plate before the appeal was made. Appeal plays are tricky. We can get into a world of different scenarios on plays like that."

A variation on the play: bases loaded, all three men tag up on a deep drive, two men are able to score on the play, but, once more, the runner off first base left early. Does one run score or two? The answer here, said Bruce Doane who has umpired since 1974, is both men score as, once again, they did so before the appeal was made. "An appeal play is a time play unless it's a force play and there was no force out there."

Now if both the runner from second and the man off first had left early and the defense appealed correctly, only one run would count.

To take the original scenario one wild leap further, could the defense, seeing they had no play on the runner who had tagged from third, appeal that the runner from first had left early and do this before the play was dead? That is to say, after the outfielder had made his catch and all three runners tagged, the defense threw not to the plate where the runner from second was about to score, but to first base a moment *before* the runner who had been on second could score. At that point the defense announced they were appealing there for the third out. Would that out prevent the second run from scoring? Umpires call such wild plays and speculations "stump the ump" questions. Culbreth stated, "It is far-fetched, but if it happened, if you appeal and if you do a legal appeal, then, yes, you could stop a run from scoring."

Of course, he added that the appeal must be done properly. For instance, "You just can't inadvertently step on a base and have that be considered as an appeal." He gave an example in which a second baseman took a cutoff from a right fielder throwing from deep down the line and as the second baseman made his throw to the plate he accidentally stepped on first base—that would not constitute an appeal, so any runner who had missed that bag could not be declared out. "When you appeal, you have to acknowledge that you're making an appeal," and you have to specify which runner you're making the appeal on.

The key for runners is simply to touch every base. "Nobody is relieved of touching a base. Nobody."

Culbreth added that weird plays seldom take place and that umpires "hope they never come along," but the thought of being on the diamond when something like an unassisted triple play or rule book puzzler takes place "is both exciting and scary at the same moment. The truth is some of these plays require not only a great knowledge of the rule book, but when these kind of plays come up—and they come up so rarely—you're still expected to rule on them just like the fact that you get four balls and three strikes, and in truth it's just not that easy to do because it's something you just don't see everyday so it takes a little bit of time for your mind to kind of register what it just saw and then put together the ruling that goes with it."

Incidentally, in 1955, *three* men tagged up on a fly to the out- field and each one scored on a sac fly. In addition, this happened in games twice within a month. Strangely enough, these rarities both took place in the same league, the Class D Appalachian League. In the first instance, outfielder Johnny Charles of Kingsport snagged a fly ball off the bat of Johnny Liprando of Bluefield, then got tangled up in a hedge that ran along center field, giving the runners ample time to scamper around the base paths. In the other case, Wytheville's Joe Oxendine got credit for his three runs driven in when Bristol center fielder Jimmy Flanagan was knocked unconscious after making a catch then running into the wall.

(40) Once it touched the pitcher in fair territory, the ball is both alive and fair. When it flew into the stands, the play had to be treated just as if, for instance, it had been a fly ball to the outfield which had then hopped into the stands—the umpires gave Ryal a ground rule double on the play.

Kuroda was released from the hospital the following day, shaken, but apparently on his way to full recovery. He stated he felt lucky to be alive and complained only of a little dizziness and a mild head-ache.

This situation, with the ball hitting the player then going into foul territory, is not the same as a famous scenario which has a ball striking off the pitcher's rubber then bounding into foul territory. In that case because the ball never went beyond first or third base and never was touched by a player, the ball is foul just as if it had hit, say, a pebble near a foul line then crossed into foul grounds before passing first or third.

"It all has to do with what is the criteria of a fair or foul ball," elucidated Sal Giacomantonio, an ump with twenty years of experience. "The criteria of a ball when ruling fair is where it crosses first or third base [and] where it settles or stops—basically if it's on the chalk line, it's fair, or where it's touched by a fielder."

41 The runner is out. As Giacomantonio related, "The first baseman was still considered to have control of the ball, to have firm and secure possession of the ball. He could pull the ball out or show the glove to show that he has the ball."

42 A do-over in baseball is virtually unheard of. As a matter of fact, the proper call here is Butler is out.

In fact, it would not have been interference even if the umpire had made contact with a catcher which may have prevented him from fielding a ball. Big league umpire Fieldin Culbreth explained, "That's not interference there. The only kind of interference you're going to have as far as me and the catcher is with him throwing the ball. Anything else kind of falls into the category of, 'Look, I've got to be out on the field, too.' If he happens to step on my foot while he's going to field that bunt, then that's just tough luck. There's no provision in the rule book to cover for that. I got to be out there and I'm trying my best to stay out of your way, but sometimes there's a chance we might make a little contact and that's unfortunate.

"There are players and personnel that have a right to be on the field, just like a photographer. He has the right to be on the field; they can put provisions in there of what he has to try to do so he doesn't become part of the game. The first base coach, the third base coach—there are provisions as to what they have to do to have [their actions] not be interference because the truth is the game has allowed them to be on the field.

"So if the ball's popped up around first base and the coach just stands his ground and the fielder runs over him, that's interference. However, if there's a ball popped up to first base and the first base coach is trying his best to avoid [the fielder] and then they end up tripping over each other, then it's tough luck."

43 Once the batter passed the runner who had just left first base, he was out so there is no force play at second. Had the defender who took the throw from the outfield applied a tag to the lead runner, it would have completed an odd twin killing, but by merely stepping on the base, he lost his shot at a double play.

44 The runner is awarded two bases because a fielder threw it out of play. As Giacomantonio explained, "It's not interference [on the batter] as long as he's standing in the box and not doing anything to [cause the contact]. The catcher just didn't give himself enough room to clear the batter to throw it." Had the ball hit the bat and deflected into fair territory, the ball is alive and a runner (or runners) could try to advance at their own risk.

(45) Giacomantonio stated, "Nine times out of ten you could probably put that runner at second and nobody's going to say a word, but the correct ruling is it's two bases from the time of the throw. So the runner that barely got back to first actually goes all the way to third." It's the same basic rule as the one in the previous question.

(46) "Duke" Rash fielded this one. "We would try not to ask for the lights until both teams had their turn at bat. At the start of the next inning is when we'd ask that the lights be turned on. But, at the same time, if it got too dark, we didn't want anybody getting hurt. We had no other recourse. We'd call the managers together and say, 'I'm sorry, but we're going to have these lights turned on.'" The same thing holds true when ordering the tarp rolled out onto the field. An umpire does not want to give either team, say the one with the lead or the team trying to play catch up, an advantage, but he does have to do what he feels is proper given the weather and the field conditions.

JUSTIN VERLANDER

OBSCURE RULES AND SITUATIONS

Ask a dozen umpires what they feel is the most difficult play for them to call correctly and, while you may not get twelve different responses, you will probably get ten varying scenarios.

American League ump Bill Kinnamon once said for him the toughest call was "throwing a guy out of a game after you blew the hell out of the play."

Cal Hubbard disagreed, saying a play at second, such as a steal, involving a sliding runner and a tag was the most difficult. "You can see it coming, but you don't know which way the runner is going to slide, where the throw is going to be, and how the fielder is going to take the throw."

Interestingly, in addition to umpiring, Hubbard was with the Green Bay Packers and had three championship titles under his belt. He is also the answer to a famous trivia question—who is the first man to be inducted into three Hall of Fames? He was honored in Cooperstown, and by the College and Pro Football Halls of Fame.

Minor league umpire "Duke" Rash said a very difficult call is "a high pitch, half swing. It's a tough call to make because the catcher is right up in front of you and sometimes you get blocked out. So you have to ask for help from your partner."

Then there's the swipe tag, not only one of the toughest plays for umps, but it is also a play that, on some occasions, requires them to rely upon a trick. In a John Kuenster article in *Baseball Digest,* Tim Welke spoke of how he realized he had missed a play in the 2008 World Series. Philadelphia's swift Jimmy Rollins was on third base and Chase Utley was on first when Ryan Howard hit a ball to Tampa pitcher Andy Sonnanstine, who began a rundown play between third and home on Rollins. Eventually third baseman Evan Longoria tagged Rollins on his derriere, but Welke, unable to see the sweep tag well, called Rollins safe. Now, here's the umpiring trick that usually works, but failed this time: "A lot of times on a swipe tag, the glove will pause [upon making contact with a runner] ... I never saw the glove pause."

Tyler Bolick and Ed Rogers, who worked as an umpiring duo in the South Atlantic League in 1999, pointed out some difficulties unique to the minors. "The toughest play for us," said Bolick, "is the check swing with the umpire's position being from the middle [of the field]." He was referring to the fact that in the majors a check swing appeal ruling is made by an umpire on first or third, gazing at a good angle towards the hitter. With a two-man crew, the umpire in the field doesn't have such an angle.

Rogers said that it's tough when the pitched ball hits a player's hands with the hands "not being part of the bat." He said, "The sound of hands being hit can sound like wood, and you say, 'What'd it hit?'" Plus, of course, he must make the call immediately.

He also felt that a "home run with fans reaching over the fence, fan interference" is an enormous challenge at any level.

Bolick added yet another demanding play: "The steal of home. You gotta call the pitch, possible interference by the catcher or batter, a balk if the pitcher speeds up his motion, and if the runner is safe or out."

Finally, there's Ryan Burich, who has umpired at every level from Little League to high school and some college ball and on up to the Northwoods League, a collegiate, wooden-bat, summer league in the Minnesota–Wisconsin area which is run like the minor leagues. He began his training when he was just sixteen. He said that for him the toughest calls came "in a two-man system—stealing bases. It's because you can't really get close to the play, you have to get an angle and some distance to the play where you can call it, and you can also have the phantom tag."

He added a pickoff of a runner off first base against a left-handed pitcher as yet another tough call. "As a base umpire you cannot tell, most of the time, if that front leg is going straight to the base or to the home plate area." Again, with a two-man system, his position is on the infield grass, not right by first base, because he has to be able to cover, say, a force play or stolen base at second as well as watching first base. "You're about eight to ten feet away from the pitcher and you don't have a good angle at seeing first base."

If you think the umpires mentioned above have it rough, brace yourself—your scenarios will get more difficult in this section, but umpires are used to that. Often things aren't clear cut in baseball. For instance, one umpire said that while the strike zone is very clearly defined by the rules, "it's more difficult than that 'cause that thing [home plate] has four corners and height, and the baseball is traveling 98 to 100 miles per hour."

YOU'RE THE UMPIRE

Before you dig into this section on obscure plays, here's one bit of very obscure umpire trivia. Major league home plate umpires squatted a grand total of 723,215 times in 2008, an average of 9,273 squats per each full-time ump. The leader that season was Alfonso Marquez with "11,254 squats in his 35 plate assignments," according to MLB.com, "including the postseason. He averaged 321.5 squats per game."

At any rate, in this, the final section, you are truly put to the test with some puzzling rules and bizarre situations. For some reason most fans find the infield fly rule to be Byzantine in its complexity. Perhaps this is so because there are so many "clauses" to the rule. The rule is in effect under certain circumstances, but not others. Likewise, many amateur umpires have been known to blow the rule concerning when a batter may attempt to reach first base on a third strike not caught cleanly by the catcher. So, again, read carefully, consider all factors, and make the call.

◌ ◌ ◌

(1) It seems fitting to start out the section dealing with rare and unusual situations and rules with an event which seems so unlikely as to be hypothetical, yet happened once in an actual big league game, an All-Star Game, nonetheless.

The date is July 8, 1997, and the scene is the mid-summer show-case at Jacobs Field in Cleveland. The top half of the second inning quickly rolled around and Seattle's fireballing southpaw, Randy

Johnson, was on the hill for the American League when hard-hitting Larry Walker of the Montreal Expos stepped up to the plate.

Background information: at the time, Walker, a left-handed out-fielder, was leading the NL in hitting at a lusty .398. As a rule, he batted with the enthusiasm of a teenage boy teeing off on a Whack-A-Mole. However, like most left-handers, he wanted no part of Johnson. The presence of The Big Unit on the mound was enough to make a left-handed hitter's blood run cold. In fact, a few weeks earlier, on June 13, Walker had asked out of the lineup when Johnson was scheduled to pitch against his team. This stirred up controversy and also nicely set up the impending All-Star confrontation between the two stars. Walker justified his request to sit out by saying his presence in the lineup against Johnson, creating a tough lefty-on-lefty mismatch, would certainly not help his team's chances for victory.

Prior to the All-Star game, Walker commented that he wouldn't fret over going hitless in an exhibition contest. "I can accept an 0-for," he stated. "It's not a life-or-death matter, unless I get hit by one of his pitches. Then it might be death."

Their memorable confrontation began when the intimidating six foot, ten inch Johnson unleashed a sizzling fastball several feet over Walker's head. After recovering his composure, Walker switched to the right-handed batter's box and turned his batting helmet around backwards so that the protective flap would cover the side of his head which would then be most vulnerable to a bean ball.

Now, what did Larry Barnett, who was working the plate that night, do? Is a batter permitted to switch from one side of the plate to another during an at bat?

Answer on pages **163–164**

(2) In a related, equally far-fetched, situation, what if a switch hitter came to the plate to face an ambidextrous pitcher. While there haven't been many men who could throw well with either arm—certainly not well enough to face fellow major leaguers—there have been a few.

The first batch of men to gain attention for pitching with both arms in major league contests came in the dusty pre-1900 era and included Tony Mullane, Larry Corcoran, and Larry Corcoran.

Mullane, nicknamed "The Count" and the "Apollo of the Box," was a Cork, Ireland, native who could also hit both ways—he hit better than .300 four years in a row, topped by a .333 season. He usually threw righty, and managed to win thirty or more contests five straight years, going 35–15 in 1883. A 284-game winner, he was the first man to pitch with both arms in a game, doing so on July 18, 1882, for Louisville against Baltimore, losing on a two-out home run in the ninth inning.

Next came Chicago pitcher Corcoran who, on June 16, 1884, used both arms from the start of the game against Buffalo due to a sore throwing (right) hand. A 177-game winner, he lasted just four innings and his team went on to lose a 20–9 blowout. Eleven days later, though, he came back with his third no-hitter.

Chamberlain was only five feet, nine inches tall and 168 pounds, but he was nicknamed "The Icebox," making him an earlier and much smaller embodiment of the NFL's William "The Refrigerator" Perry. At any rate, Chamberlain pitched both ways on May 9, 1888, for Louisville in an 18–6 laugher over Kansas City. Enjoying a huge lead he threw the last two innings of the game lefty, giving up half of his eight hits over that stretch. He would go on to win 159 games during his career.

As recently as 1995, Greg Harris, normally a right-handed pitcher, threw with both arms in a game for the Montreal Expos against the Cincinnati Reds. Harris had always wanted to do this—in fact, he had obtained a glove specially designed so it could easily be slipped on either hand, permitting him to use the other arm to throw the ball. Then, in a meaningless game near the end of the season—his Expos began the September 28 contest some twenty four-and-half games behind the division-leading Atlanta Braves—he finally got the opportunity to display his ambidexterity.

He entered the game in the top of the ninth inning with the Reds up 9–3. He induced Reggie Sanders to ground out to the shortstop. Then, switching to the use of his left arm, he walked Hal Morris and retired Eddie Taubensee, a left-handed hitter like Morris, on a ball hit near the plate for an easy out. Switching hands again, he got Bret

Boone to hit a tapper which he fielded for another routine out. The inning was over with Harris recording a nearly perfect line in the box score for his most unusual appearance. He would pitch, exclusively right-handed, just one more game that year and then his big league career was through.

Prior to Harris the last major leaguer to use both arms was a Brooklyn pitcher with the poetic name of Ed Head. In the 1940s, he once pitched with both arms against the Cubs in Wrigley Field. *Baseball Digest* reported he did so briefly, in just one inning, "after injuring his right arm," throwing "a number of pitches with his left arm in a 9–7 loss to Cincinnati."

So just what would happen if an ambidextrous pitcher was working in a game when a switch hitter came to the plate? Would a farce ensue with the pitcher, for example, getting ready to throw lefty to a left-handed hitter only to have the batter call time and move to the other box? After his move would the pitcher then simply switch his glove to his other hand in preparation to throw righty now? This crazy dance could go on and on ad infinitum so there must be a rule to cover the situation, right? What action must an umpire take here?

Answer on page **164**

(3) During a game between Cleveland and Minnesota on August 16, 2006, Jason Michaels of the Indians struck out on *two* strikes, not three. Michaels led off the eighth and took three pitches from Twins

hurler Dennys Reyes in a 2–2 tie. Thinking incorrectly that home plate ump, Rob Drake, had called the first pitch a strike, even though he never indicated such, Michaels saw two more pitches and, when they were both strikes, he retired to the dugout. Catcher Joe Mauer knew the count was really 1–2, but wisely kept mum, as did Drake. "I wasn't going to say anything," Mauer quipped. Not a single member of the Indians caught the mistake, leading Cleveland manager Eric Wedge to later comment tersely and lamentably, "That's a first." How should have this situation been handled?

Answer on page **165**

(4) It's the 1975 World Series and the Cincinnati Reds are taking on the Boston Red Sox in a classic. Each team had won a contest when Game Three rolls around, and that game is tied at five runs apiece in the bottom of the tenth inning. The tension is as palpable as fear in a foxhole.

Pinch hitter Ed Armbrister squares to lay down a bunt to advance Cesar Geronimo, who had opened the inning with a single to right field, into scoring position. The bunt hits near home plate and takes a high hop not far from Red Sox catcher Carlton Fisk. Leaping from his spot behind the plate in order to field the ball, Fisk bumps into, and gets tangled up with, Armbrister, who is attempting to get a good jump out of the right-handers' box. When Fisk finally extricates himself from the two-man pile up, his throw to second for the force goes wild, into center field for an error. Geromino makes it to third: Armbrister reaches second.

However, before you allow them to do so, consider all the factors—are the runners, in fact, entitled to second and third? It seems the contact between batter and catcher was unavoidable, but does that exonerate Armbrister or does his action constitute interference?

Answer on pages **165–166**

(5) Here's an old and odd one. In the hazy, pre-1900 days of baseball, some rules were different than those of what we have today and some rules which we now have weren't even conceived of back then. Mike "King" Kelly, who played from 1878 to 1893 and is said to have invented the slide, was known for his cleverness. One day he was on the bench when an opponent lofted a foul ball Kelly's way. Realizing no teammate had a chance to make a play of the popper, he bellowed out, "Kelly now catching," leapt from his seat, and caught the ball. Can this possibly be a legal catch?

Answer on page **166**

(6) Imagine the Texas Rangers have runners leading off first and second base and they still have nobody out. Respected hitter Michael Young is at the plate, but this time, fooled badly, he misconnects on an 0–2 curve and pops it to the backpedaling Jack Wilson at shortstop for

Seattle. It's an obvious situation for the infield fly rule until the wind, billowing straight out, nudges the ball into the area which can typically be covered by an infielder *or* by an outfielder—very shallow left field. There, left fielder Ryan Langerhans comes in on the ball but somehow drops what should have been a routine out. Once the ball was beyond the dirt of the infield and was touched by an outfielder is the infield fly rule waved off?

Answer on pages **166–169**

(7) The date was May 27, 1981, and third baseman Lenny Randle did something which led to his becoming a fixture on blooper tapes. The game was in the top of the seventh inning when the Royals sent Amos Otis to the plate. He hit a dribbler down the third base line where three Seattle Mariners tentatively approached the ball and soon realized they would have no play on Otis. At that point Randle did more than just wish the ball would roll into foul territory; he got down on his hands and knees and blew the ball over the line. Technically, he never touched the ball, so can this be some sort of interference? What do you suppose home umpire Larry McCoy ruled that day?

Answer on page **169**

(8) In a Cubs versus Phillies game of September 11, 1969, pitcher Dick Selma tried a trick pickoff play with his third baseman, Ron Santo. With Phillies on first and second and a payoff pitch due with two men

out, Selma, knowing the runners would be off with the pitch, stepped off the rubber and threw to third. However, Santo had forgotten the signal and the ball shot by him into left field, ultimately costing the Cubs the game. Now, should this pickoff move have been called a balk, allowing runners to advance just one base?

Answer on pages **169–170**

(9) Another World Series scenario. This time from October 15, 1969, when the New York Mets took on the Baltimore Orioles in Game Four at Shea Stadium. The game labored on into the eleventh inning, still knotted at 1–1, when the Mets placed Jerry Grote at second on his two-base hit, a pop up that fell into short left field. Rod Gaspar entered the game to pinch run for Grote just before Al Weiss was given first base on an intentional walk. With nobody out, it was an obvious bunting situation for batter J. C. Martin.

Sure enough, he laid one down. The ball trickled near the first base foul line where it was fielded by O's pitcher Pete Richert, who decided to go for the sure out at first. However, his throw hit Martin, kicked into the outfield, and Gaspar darted home with the game-winning tally.

Does the fact that Martin was not running inside the three-foot wide lane which is marked in chalk for the last forty-five feet from home to first have any bearing on this play?

Answer on pages **170–171**

(10) A relief pitcher, say Jonathan Papelbon, enters a game with the bases empty, takes the customary eight warm-up pitches, but then, rather than work the batter, hesitates. Perhaps he meditates off the rubber à la Al Hrabosky, or perhaps he plays a cat-and-mouse game with the hitter, waiting him out. Is there, as is the case in football, some version of a delay of game call an umpire can make on a player for holding up the works as Papelbon did in this question?

Answer on pages **171–172**

(11) Paul O'Neill was playing right field one day in 1989 for the Cincinnati Reds. The game was on the line in the ninth inning and the Philadelphia Phillies had Steve Jeltz, representing the potential winning run, in scoring position. A ball was hit through the infield and into right where O'Neill, feeling rushed to get off a strong throw to the plate to snuff out the would-be game-ending run, bobbled it, juggled it, and then, out of frustration, kicked the ball. Amazingly, the ball shot directly to Todd Benzinger, his cutoff man at first base; the befuddled base runner had to hold up at third. It's your call—does the play stand or is there a penalty for O'Neill's actions here?

Answer on page **172**

(12) The year is 1960 and the Pittsburgh Pirates have the bases loaded with two men out. On a full count the runners know the "merry-go-round" play is on—since the next pitch will either end the inning on

a strikeout, result in a walk, or the ball will be placed into action—and they all take off on the pitch. Dick Groat's grounder to Philadelphia second baseman Tony Taylor is fielded smoothly. Taylor then extends his arms to tag Don Hoak, the runner off first; Hoak veers out of base line to avoid the tag and thus is automatically out. However, Bill Mazeroski, the runner off third, gets such a huge jump and the play near second base takes so long to develop that Maz scores before the third out is called—or did he? Do you count the run or not?

Answer on page **172**

(13) Say the Milwaukee Brewers and the Houston Astros are deadlocked in the last half of the ninth inning. With nobody out, Jeff Bagwell of the host Astros tattoos the ball, sending it to the far reaches of left field, but in foul territory. The runner off third, Craig Biggio, prepares to tag up and score the game's decisive run. Then, as the ball trails over toward the stands, a fan reaches out and makes a marvelous, though illegal, grab of the ball which clearly was over the playing field. The third base umpire rules interference, the ball is instantly dead on arrival, so to speak, and the batter is declared out. What ruling applies to the man tagging from third?

Answer on pages **172–173**

(14) Chicago Cubs left fielder Moises Alou was playing in a home game against the Astros in Wrigley Field. Houston's Adam Everett ripped

a ball that deflected off Alou's glove and came to rest in the ivy on the outfield wall. Alou quickly raised his arms, the traditional signal to umpires indicating a ball was lost, no longer in play. What's the ruling in this odd situation?

Answer on page **173**

(15) In a 1979 contest the Dodgers' Joe Ferguson came to the plate with the bases loaded against the Pittsburgh Pirates. The count ran full and on the next delivery, Lee Lacy, the runner off third, believed the umpire had called strike three and veered off the base path and headed toward the dugout.

Lacy's action led Pirate catcher Manny Sanguillen to believe the third out had indeed been recorded so he casually rolled the ball out toward the mound. Jim Wynn, the runner on second base, was more alert—he dashed around third and stepped on the plate. Even more confusion resulted when Lacy, still on the field, finally realized what was going on and redirected himself to home plate as well. The umpires had to huddle over this one—what was their final call to straighten out the anarchy?

Answer on page **174**

(16) Some situations aren't covered by any rule book and an umpire must improvise. "Duke" Rash, who once umpired in the minors, said that one time in a park with poor lighting "a ball was hit—I mean, really

hit—high and deep. It got up above the lights and I was watching the ball from home plate and I lost the ball in the lights. And I looked at my partner Bruce Froemming to see if he was giving me a motion of some sort [to indicate foul ball or home run], but he wasn't. He was looking up in the air and the outfielder was at the fence in fair territory by about five feet, looking straight up." From the meager input he had to go on, what do you suppose Rash ruled and why?

Answer on page **174**

(17) Say the Los Angeles Dodgers are playing the Cincinnati Reds and the free-spirited Jay Johnstone reaches first on a crisp single to right-center field, sending a teammate to third. He then swipes second, hoping to draw a throw from the catcher which conceivably could have led to a double steal, but no throw from the catcher ensues. Now, in an effort to rattle the pitcher or, strange as it sounds, set up another possible double steal, on the next pitch Johnstone "steals" first, retreating to that bag without a throw being made. Is this legal?

Answer on pages **174–175**

(18) As recently as August 23, 2008, an odd play involving a third strike not being caught by a catcher took place. With two men out, Melvin Mora of the Orioles was at the plate with a 1–2 count. The runner off first base, Nick Markakis, took off on the pitch, which Mora whiffed on. However, Yankees catcher Ivan Rodriguez did not come up with

the ball, which had hit in the dirt, cleanly. Nor did he remember to tag Mora, who, with two outs (even with a man on first), was entitled to try to reach first base before "Pudge" could apply a tag or throw him out at first base.

Mora began to walk out of the dirt area which surrounds the plate and trudged toward his dugout. Suddenly, informed of what was going on, Mora made his belated way for first. Now it was the Yankees defense's turn to become oblivious—believing the third out had been chalked up, they jogged off the field.

The two Baltimore runners advanced two bases to second and third before New York manager Joe Girardi pled his case. What argument could he make here and what did the umps do about it?

Answer on page **176**

(19) The Dodgers hosted the Diamondbacks on April 12, 2009, when the "fourth out" rule came into play. In the second inning, Andre Ethier was camped out at third base, Juan Pierre was at second, and one Dodger was out. Pitcher Randy Wolf ripped a Dan Haren pitch right back to the box. The pitcher stabbed the ball, leaving both Ethier (who had made his break for home on the contact play) and Pierre off their respective bases with insufficient time to return to safety. Haren fired to second where Felipe Lopez was covering. Had Lopez stomped on second base to complete an inning-ending double play, the umpires wouldn't have had to clear up a muddled situation. However, Lopez ran over to Pierre, by then between second and third, and tagged him for out number three. By that time Ethier had stepped on home plate, even as the Diamondback defenders trotted off the field—after all, there were three outs, so what's the problem? The fact is, there was a very big problem. Your question is this: did Ethier's run count?

Answer on pages **176–177**

(20) On the final day of the 1950 season the Brooklyn Dodgers played host to the Philadelphia Phillies, with the pennant on the line. If Brooklyn, trailing the "Whiz Kids" by one game in the standings, won they would force a playoff situation. However, if they lost, it was all over and the Phillies could hoist the pennant. Starting pitchers, the aces of their respective staffs, Don Newcombe of Brooklyn and Robin Roberts of Philadelphia, were both trying to nail down their twentieth win of the year.

In the bottom half of the sixth inning Brooklyn's Pee Wee Reese lifted a fly ball which miraculously landed, and *stayed*, on top of the fence which was secured to the middle of a thick wall. The ball was in play and Reese was therefore free to romp around the bases.

Catcher Andy Seminick yelled for right fielder Del Ennis to fire his glove at the ball to dislodge it, but Ennis was unable to hear his teammate over the din of the excited crowd.

If Ennis had thought of throwing his glove at the ball and if it had struck the ball, what would the umpires have done about it?

Answer on pages **177–178**

OBSCURE RULES AND SITUATIONS

(21) This brain-wracking situation took place on May 17, 2009, in a game between Cleveland and Tampa Bay. Rays manager Joe Maddon erred by listing two of his players as the game's third basemen, while neglecting to name his designated hitter anywhere on his lineup card. What he intended was to have Ben Zobrist play third that game and to have Evan Longoria in the DH spot. Once Maddon turned over his lineup card to the umpires, he was doomed, forced to live with his mistake. What penalty did his team incur?

Answer on pages **178–181**

(22) Here's another batting-out-of-order situation—this one came just three days after the above dilemma. On May 20, the Astros, for the first time in team history, sent the wrong man to the plate when manager Cecil Cooper notified his players of his batting order, but then turned in a different lineup card to the umpires. Michael Bourn, who should have hit in the number-two slot, led off and singled through the right side of the infield against the Brewers. Kaz Matsui then began to approach the batter's box, but he was the player who was written in on the official card as the leadoff hitter. Milwaukee manager Ken Macha then strolled out to the home plate ump and pointed out the infraction to him. What occurred next?

Answer on page **181**

23 The 1980 NLCS pitted the Houston Astros against the Philadelphia Phillies in a stellar best-of-five affair that went the distance. Drama prevailed as each of the final four games went into extra innings. The fourth game was scoreless entering the top half of the fourth inning. The Phils put two men on base via singles, Bake McBride at second and Manny Trillo at first, bringing Garry Maddox to the plate. He promptly hit a looping ball, a soft line drive, back to Houston pitcher Vern Ruhle, who seized the ball very near to the artificial turf of the Astrodome and went to first for the sure out. At that moment home plate umpire Doug Harvey declared Ruhle had trapped the ball, but the first and third base umps informed him that Ruhle had caught the ball on the fly, meaning his throw to first, catching the trailing runner off the base, completed a double play.

Having heard the ball was caught on the fly, Astros first baseman Art Howe, after a moment of confusion, ran the ball toward second and tagged McBride, who was still off the base, for a triple play.

The Phillies, led by manager Dallas Green, argued that their runners had been at a disadvantage, believing initially that the ball had hit the ground. The six-man umpiring crew, discussing the puzzling matter with National League President Chub Feeney, who was seated in a field level box seat that day, required twenty minutes to straighten the situation out. How would you have handled the situation?

Answer on page **182**

(24) On August 9, 2006, a contest between the Oakland A's and the Texas Rangers ended suddenly and in a rather unexpected way. With Texas pinch runner Jerry Hariston Jr. on first base and Mark DeRosa at the plate with one out, the Rangers, still trailing the A's, had rallied on a two-run single by Hank Blalock to bring them within one run of Oakland. On a payoff pitch to DeRosa, Texas manager Buck Showalter had Hariston running on the pitch from A's closer Huston Street knowing that a gap shot could possibly tie the game up. DeRosa whiffed, but Hairston slid safely into the second base bag. However, home plate umpire Jim Joyce announced that DeRosa's action as he struck out resulted in two outs. The game, said Joyce, was over. What did DeRosa do to cause the Rangers to be charged with those outs to end the game?

Answer on page **182**

(25) The Reds were in Los Angeles on August 1, 1971, when, in the eleventh inning of a game knotted at 4–4, Willie Crawford came to the plate. There were two men out and the Dodgers had loaded the bases against relief pitcher Joe Gibbon. Manny Mota led off third and decided he had a chance to end the game with a dramatic steal of home. Cincinnati catcher Johnny Bench saw the play unfolding and leapt from his spot in the catcher's box, going up the third base line a tad, ready to catch the ball and slap his tag on Mota. What did the umpire declare on this play?

Answer on pages **182–183**

26 The year was 2008 and Larry Bowa was working the third base coaching box for the Dodgers. Umpire Ed Montague told him to put on a protective helmet. Bowa refused. As a matter of fact, he argued vehemently with the ump. Did Montague have the authority to make Bowa wear a helmet?

Answer on pages **183–185**

27 Say Milwaukee Brewers outfielder Ryan Braun is on third base and Prince Fielder has just reached first in a game against the Cubs. One man is out when Mike Cameron lifts a fly ball to deep left where Alfonso Soriano hauls it down. Braun tags up but Fielder, running on what he felt was a sure extra base hit, is doubled off first. Now Braun, running furiously, crossed home plate a few ticks of the clock sooner than the third out on Fielder was recorded. Does that matter? Does the run count or not?

Answer on page **185**

28 In 1997 Matt Williams won a Gold Glove in his only season as the third baseman of the Cleveland Indians. He was as slick with the glove as he was with the ball—the old hidden ball, that is. On September 19 of that year he decided to try and pull off the good ol' hidden ball trick during a game against Kansas City Royals, choosing their second baseman Jed Hansen as his victim.

Believe it or not, Williams simply asked Hansen to step off the base for a moment so he could clean it, and the youngster, who had just stolen third and started a casual conversation with third base coach Rich Dauer, complied, falling for the housecleaning request ploy. "I was gullible enough to step off," confessed the then-twenty-five-year-old. "It took me totally by surprise. I was not paying attention. It won't happen again."

Cleveland catcher Sandy Alomar recalled that Williams "told the guy to get off the base so he could clean it. He was a rookie. Williams tagged the guy and he was out; they were pretty upset about that." The Royals were so irate, in fact, that the next inning when Williams came to bat he was drilled by a pitch.

The crafty Williams explained the nuances of the play, "It was sort of a spur-of-the-moment thing. I wasn't trying to embarrass anyone." Williams had just received the throw from catcher Pat Borders on the successful steal. He then feigned a lob back to pitcher Brian Anderson, while he actually threw the ball into his own glove.

He then showed the ball to the ump to alert him as to what was about to happen. Williams, who had spent his entire career prior to 1997 in the National League, did that as a precaution. "I've noticed," he said, "that the umpires in this league call time out a lot." If the ump had done that, the play would have been dead right then and there. A few seconds later he applied the tag and the rare play had worked.

Aside from an umpire calling a time out, there is a second big stumbling block in pulling off this play. Can you identify the rule involving the pitcher, a rule which every umpire must know, concerning this trick play?

Answer on pages **185–186**

(29) The Pittsburgh Pirates were taking on the Chicago Cubs in 1992 when an odd play took place. Pittsburgh's Kirk Gibson was off and motoring from first base on a hit and run play when Jay Bell slapped the ball on the ground to the right side of the infield. Incredibly, the ball hit Gibson's batting helmet which had bounced off his head as he made his mad dash for second base. The ball was then redirected toward the second base bag where Ryne Sandberg, about to cover that base, picked it up and threw it to third to trigger a run down on the shocked Gibson—after all, hadn't he just seen that the ball clearly was on a path to send it into right field? Ultimately Gibson was retired on the run down, but will that call stand or will you overturn it? Is the ball still in play after hitting a piece of detached equipment?

Answer on page **187**

(30) Johnny Damon is stationed in left field for the Yankees in this scenario. The bases are loaded for the Kansas City Royals and only one man is out. Damon takes off in pursuit of a twisting fly ball down the line, making a grab for it while both feet are in foul territory. Then,

after making a great grab, he tumbles into the stands. Explain all the ramifications of this play starting with this—is it a legal catch for an out?

Answer on page **187**

(31) Juan Marichal, a man who threw a twelve-strikeout one-hitter in his first big league outing, then breezed into the Hall of Fame in 1983, some 242 additional victories later, is on the hill in this imaginary setting. The "Dominican Dandy" looks over at third base where the speedy and daring Maury Wills leads off. Marichal has two outs on the Dodgers so he decides to work out of his windup, featuring his patented high leg kick, to big Frank Howard. Wills, believing the best chance for Los Angeles to score is a steal of home, times Marichal then bolts for the plate. Just as Wills slides into home he is struck by the pitch that was actually just inside the strike zone. Now, since the count on the batter was full, what's your ruling? What do you do with Howard and with Wills?

Answer on page **187**

(32) Another imaginary problem. Brian Roberts of the Baltimore Orioles is on first base with one man already retired. Adam Jones lifts a lazy pop up to Craig Counsell who is playing second base for the Milwaukee Brewers. The wily veteran decides to allow the ball to fall at his feet, and he then pounces on the ball and fires to shortstop J. J. Hardy,

who completes the double play by firing the ball to Prince Fielder at first. Is there a rule to prevent such chicanery?

Answer on page **188**

(33) This one has to be among the most bizarre plays in the history of baseball and you can bet there is absolutely no way the rule book covered it, at least not specifically, not exactly like this play took place, simply because there had never been a play like it in the history of pro ball.

During a minor league contest on August 31, 1987, Williamsport catcher Dave Bresnahan, (great-nephew of one of the greatest catchers of all time, Roger Bresnahan) concocted a most unconventional scheme.

He knew he would have to wait until an opposing team had a runner on third base to unveil his plan. So, when a runner from the opposing Reading team had chugged home, and another runner, Rick Lundblade, dropped anchor at third, Bresnahan was prepared to make history.

He requested time out from the home plate umpire, pretending that he needed a new catcher's mitt. Now, what Lundblade did not suspect—and, for that matter, what nobody in the park could envision—was the fact that the new glove had, of all things, a peeled potato hidden inside. As the next pitch came in to Bresnahan, he clutched the potato in his bare hand (or, to employ a pun, his "meat and potato" hand). Then, remarkably, and quite intentionally, he threw the vegetable wildly, like a hot potato, beyond third base and into the left field.

Lundblade saw a white blur whiz by and, naturally, assumed it was the ball—after all, one simply doesn't expect to see a potato soaring around a ball field. Therefore, he proceeded to streak toward home plate.

Bresnahan, of course, was waiting there for him, baseball in hand. One imagines an evil grin on his face as he tagged the runner out in a sort of "Now you see it, now you see it *again*" bit of sleight of hand. How would you attempt to straighten out the situation here?

Answer on pages **188–190**

(34) In the final inning of a 10–0 blowout with the Seattle Mariners trailing the visiting Cleveland Indians, Jack Hannahan, the M's third baseman, was hit by a pitch. The next batter, Rob Johnson, slashed a double down the right field line, which wound up in the stands for, what was officially scored a double. Instead of advancing the normal two bases on such a play, Hannahan was permitted to score the first of Seattle's three runs of the game. Why? What could the umpire have seen which made his give Hannahan another base? (Clue: It involves a rule dealt with earlier in this book.)

Answer on pages **190–191**

35 Here's one that is very rarely seen. St. Louis was playing in Philadelphia's Citizen Bank Park on July 26, 2009, when the always-dangerous Chase Utley came to the plate in the bottom half of the first inning. Philly was down 1–0, but had the speedy Shane Victorino, "The Flyin' Hawaiian," at first base. Phillies manager Charlie Manuel decided to shake things up a bit by running Victorino. So, on a 1–0 pitch from Todd Wellemeyer, he sent Victorino who got such a great jump he virtually cruised into second base. However, on the play Cardinal catcher Jason LaRue's throwing hand made contact with the face mask of home plate ump Brian O'Nora, forcing him to fumble around with the ball and ultimately preventing him from getting a throw off.

If you were O'Nora, what would your call be? What do you do with Victorino and what do you do with the count on Utley?

Answer on pages **191–192**

36 Bobby Bragan recalled an odd play which occurred when the home plate ump left his spot to hustle down to cover third while the third base umpire, who had gone away from his position momentarily, returned, following the ball to third where a play was then being made. Bragan remembered, "One umpire called a runner safe and the other one called it out." How do umpires straighten out such a quagmire of a problem?

Answer on pages **193–195**

OBSCURE RULES AND SITUATIONS

(37) A handful of players such as Barry Bonds and Brady Anderson wore protective elbow padding. (Some said in Bonds's case it was more like a piece of armor for his right arm, the one exposed to the pitcher.) Can any player, perhaps a man trying to get an edge by wearing a ton of padding so he could better crowd the plate without fearing the pitcher would reclaim the inner part of the plate by hitting him, decide to add padding or are there restrictions to prevent this?

Answer on page **196**

(38) A pitcher, let's say Houston ace Roy Oswalt, is working out of the stretch with a runner on first base. While peering in to get his sign from the catcher, he accidentally drops the baseball. As the home plate umpire what, if anything, do you call?

Answer on page **196**

(39) What about this: Once again with a man on first base, Oswalt comes to a full stop at the belt, begins his motion, then for whatever reason— perhaps he got confused and wasn't sure which pitch his catcher had just called for or the batter stepped out on him, upsetting his rhythm—he hesitates or stops instead of throwing the ball, wanting to reset before going through with his next pitch. Is his movement legal or illegal?

Answer on pages **196–197**

(40) A base runner, let's say A. J. Pierzynski, gets picked off first base by Chad Billingsley in interleague action. He gets hung up in a run down and winds up just a few yards away from second base where shortstop Rafael Furcal stands in the base path, blocking his way. Trying to reach the base, Pierzynski makes some contact with Furcal a second or so before he catches the ball and applies a tag. Pierzynski's actions seem just a bit suspicious—as if he perhaps bumped into the defender on purpose, that he could easily have avoided contact.

As the umpire do you punish the defense and allow the runner to return with no risk to first base? Is this a judgment play where the ump has the authority to call Pierzynski out—either for making contact initially or by assuming he certainly was destined to be out on the play anyway? Just what is the proper call?

Answer on page **197**

(41) Same situation and same circumstances. The only difference is that this time Pierzynski is heading back to first base in an effort to escape his pickle of a situation. This time he initiates contact with James Loney, who, like Furcal, did not have the ball yet. Is the ruling different than in question 40 because he was going back to his original base and not moving on to the next one?

Answer on pages **197–198**

42 Assume there are runners on first and second with one man out and there's a count of 1–2 on Jeff Francoeur of the New York Mets. The next pitch strikes him out but the ball plunged into the dirt near home plate. The opposing catcher, St. Louis Cardinals Gold Glove winner Yadier Molina, decides that because he didn't catch strike three cleanly he has to tag Francoeur. However, by that time the Mets outfielder is darting for first base. Molina's throw to retire the runner at first takes off deep into the right field corner, permitting two runs to score and Francoeur to settle on reaching second base. Do you, the crew chief, allow things to play out that way or not?

Answer on pages **198–199**

43 Here's an odd one from 2009: The Rays were taking on the Red Sox in St. Petersburg, Florida, when a ball bag which was frequently placed next to the Rays' bullpen near the right field foul line came into play and almost cost Tampa Bay a ball game all because of their poor housekeeping.

Ben Zobrist was on first for the Rays with nobody out in the eighth inning of a 2–2 game. Boston relief pitcher Daniel Bard gloved a bunt by Willy Aybar and threw it wildly down the line. Somehow the ball took a bounce and landed directly in a bullpen ball bag. Right fielder J. D. Drew raised his arm, signaling to the umps that the ball had gone out of play as Zobrist was steaming around third, soon to score a key run. Moments later, Aybar, never breaking stride, also crossed home. What did the umpires rule on this play?

Answer on pages **199–201**

(44) Cameron Castro was playing in a game for Lake Erie College when "the opposing catcher had a passed ball with a runner on first. He scoops the ball up with his mask." At that point the umpire made a call on "a rule I was unaware of.... You never see it." What was that call?

Answer on page **201**

(45) Roberto Alomar said he played in a game once (not in the majors) in which a runner led off first and just as the pitcher threw over on a pickoff toss, a teammate of the pitcher sitting in the dugout took a ball and threw it down the right field line. The runner, seeing the ball scoot away, believed the pitcher threw wildly so he jumped up and began his race for second only to be tagged by the first baseman still holding the game ball. While Alomar said the ump that day let the play stand—perhaps he didn't see the other ball thrown onto the field—it is clearly illegal. If you were the ump what would you do to rectify this injustice?

Answer on page **202**

(46) Bruce Doane was working a college game between Western Michigan and Michigan once when runners were on first and third and

"the guy's stealing second and they throw to second base. Well, the shortstop cuts the ball off and throws home to try to retire the runner that's coming from third base." By then second base was easily stolen. The batter then interfered with the catcher, who was trying to catch the ball and tag the runner out. What do you do with the two runners and how do you sort out this mess?

Answer on page **202**

(47) Doane was working another game around 2005 when "we were emphasizing the pitcher not coming to a complete stop [prior to making a pitch]. A left-hander was on the mound [with runners off first and third] and he bounced [his hand, never coming to a stop] and I thought he was coming home. Well, he threw to first base. I yelled out, 'Balk.' Then I go, 'No, that's not a balk.' Well the guy on first base got picked off—they got him in a rundown and the runner from third scored. Now I've got myself a big argument." How did Doane extricate himself from his plight?

Answer on pages **202–203**

(48) Atlanta manager Bobby Cox, who holds the record for being tossed from more games over a career than any other skipper, is in his dugout when the home plate umpire makes what Cox believes to be a terrible call against Braves star Chipper Jones, ringing him up on strikes. Enraged, Cox charges the ump to squawk about the

ball-strike call. If he watches his temper and his language, is Cox in any peril of racking up yet another ejection?

Answer on page **203**

(49) During a 2009 interview, Jamey Carroll of the Cleveland Indians spoke of a peculiar play which took place that season. He was a bit hazy about the particulars, but said the other team's first baseman was off the bag when he took a throw on what Carroll seems to recall was a bunt play. While he then tried to tag the runner coming down the line, the runner "avoided the tag, but missed first base, went past first base. And our guy [then] stepped on the base." The runner then went back to the bag, but is it too late, is he out? What's your call here?

Answer on pages **203–205**

(50) The date is June 30, 1959. Cubs' pitcher Bob Anderson had a full count on Cardinals' superstar and seven-time NL batting champ Stan Musial. The next pitch came in high and tight and soared by catcher Sammy Taylor as plate ump Vic Delmore waved Musial to first base. Taylor and Anderson, both believing the ball had nicked Musial's bat, began arguing with Delmore. Musial zipped to first about the time Taylor requested a new baseball from the ump.

Meanwhile, third baseman Alvin Dark rushed to the backstop to pick up the original baseball while Musial lit off for second base. By that point the alert Dark *and* Anderson realized they had a shot at retiring Musial so they both fired balls to shortstop Ernie Banks, who was covering the bag. Dark's throw was a low one but was gloved by Banks while Anderson's peg soared over second baseman Tony Taylor's head. Musial slid safely into second, spotted a baseball flying into the outfield, so he hopped up and prepared to set sail for third, but he didn't get far—Banks tagged him with the other ball.

Chicago argues Musial is therefore out while St. Louis contends Musial is entitled to third base due to the errant throw into the outfield. Just imagine—two balls were both live and in play at the same time. Who was correct? Take a stab at this knotty problem.

Answer on page **205**

RYAN HOWARD

ANSWERS

(1) Home plate ump Barnett did absolutely nothing—except, perhaps, chuckle over the almost surreal, yet comical scene. Like any hitter, Walker is certainly *allowed* to bat from either side of the plate, as if he really was a switch hitter. By the way, he had never before batted righty, not even for one big league pitch. The next pitch after the very wild Johnson pitch was a ball. Walker then turned around to bat lefty once more, and eventually drew a walk. American League manager Joe Torre speculated that the scenario had been pre-arranged by the two men, but he enjoyed the comedic display, nevertheless.

Many little kids believe a batter may switch during an at bat, but not after the he has two strikes on him. That's a fallacy; the count is immaterial. Of course, kids playing informal sandlot pick-up games are free to create their own rules, especially ground rules—any batter hitting a ball to the opposite field is automatically out (this comes into play when there aren't enough boys to man every position on the diamond); a ball which travels past the old sycamore tree is a home run; or any ball hit into Old Man Mueller's backyard is declared a lost ball and the batter is out.

Kids don't have to follow big league rules, but umpires do and Barnett, of course, knew Walker was free to bat lefty or righty any time he wanted to—and he *sure* wanted to go righty against the filthy offerings of Johnson.

Incidentally, the Walker–Johnson at bat was reminiscent of the John Kruk versus Randy Johnson battle, another mismatch, that one in the 1993 All-Star Game. In that case, Johnson uncorked a 98-mile per-hour fastball over Kruk's head. Kruk responded by clutching at his chest as if he had just suffered a heart attack. The result of the rest of his at bat was a given, he whiffed, bailing out badly on the next two pitches after standing so far off the plate reporters joked that he might as well have batted from his dugout.

(2) When a switch hitter faces an ambidextrous pitcher, a specific rule governs the situation. While a switch hitter has never faced an ambidextrous pitcher in a big league game, that rule states that if such a situation did come up, the man on the mound would have to indicate how he would deliver the next pitch and the hitter could then determine how he would bat, ending any further changes. If either man wanted to change on the *next* pitch, that's fine, but the batter always has the final move.

Yankees prospect Pat Venditte began pitching in the minors in 2008 and according to Wikipedia, his ambidexterity led to a new rule which declares a "pitcher [with that ability] must visually indicate to the umpire, batter, and runner(s) which way he will begin pitching to the batter."

(3) Several days after the incident in which Michaels was cheated out of a strike (and therefore cheated of a completed at bat), *The Plain Dealer* of Cleveland reported that Jim McKean, supervisor for Major League Baseball's umpires, commented Michaels should have been called back to the box. "If we knew there were two strikes, we should have gone and gotten him. It wouldn't have mattered if he was already in the dugout. It wasn't the third out of the inning.

"But once the next guy came to the plate and a pitch was thrown, that was it." Meanwhile, Michaels said he was embarrassed by the incident. "I'm extremely mad at myself. I'm kicking myself." He added, "It's all on me. It's my fault."

(4) The home plate umpire in this classic event was Larry Barnett who declared no interference on the part of Armbrister. The contact with the Boston catcher, said Barnett, was unintentional, and *that* is the key to this call. "They just collided. I felt that the guy had as much right to go to first base as the other guy had to catch the ball.... It was just a bump, and Fisk was able to pick up the ball and throw it."

While many observers disagreed, naturally, the call stood. Plus it was the correct call in that neither Armbrister nor Fisk, wrote Bruce Weber author of *As They See 'Em*, "gained or lost an advantage from what was inadvertent contact." The rule book is now written to indicate that such *unintentional* contact out in front of home plate is not to be considered interference.

To wrap things up regarding that gem of a World Series, Pete Rose was walked intentionally, Merv Rettenmund pinch hit and whiffed, and then Joe Morgan rapped a single up the middle to give the Reds a 6–5 victory over Boston. Cincinnati would go on to take the World Series in seven.

(5) According to one source, the rule book had nothing in it to stipulate a move such as Kelly made was illegal. In fact, back then the rules permitted a substitution to occur *any* time at all. However, the umpire trumped the rule book, perhaps using the logic that Kelly was making a mockery of the game, and did not allow the out to be recorded.

Umpire Ryan Burich said he loves the blanket rule which broadly empowers an ump to make a final decision on anything not covered by the rule book, calling it "a nice, little handy tool in the back pocket of an umpire to use."

(6) No. The play remains governed by the oft-misunderstood infield fly rule which states that a player's defensive position or, you might say here, his title (i.e., outfielder) doesn't matter. Because the outfielder was making the play when the infield fly had been called, the rule applies just as if the left fielder or an infielder had secured the ball. The batter is out. "It doesn't matter who caught it; the ball was caught [or, in this question, was expected to have been caught] with ordinary effort," said umpire Sal Giacomantonio. Of course, if either or both runners felt they could advance after the dropped ball, they could certainly do so at their own risk.

As ex-umpire "Duke" Rash explained, "It's a judgment call by the umpire—even though the ball's in the outfield, they can still call the infield fly rule. We'd have to yell [to avoid any possible confusion], 'Infield fly rule. The batter's out.'" It doesn't even matter if an infielder is in the outfield with his back to the infield, an umpire can still call for this rule to be in effect.

Fieldin Culbreth explained more about the rule. Would an umpire, for example, consider almost any pop up to be a routine out when, say, an Omar Vizquel in his prime was chasing after it? Culbreth said the skill level of the fielder going for the ball has no bearing on his calling the infield fly rule. "When you start bringing names into it, I can assure you the answer is no. It has nothing to do with Omar Vizquel, no more than if you had the glove in your hand. It has every-thing to do with when [a fielder] is underneath that baseball and I think that you have got yourself positioned to catch it with ordinary effort, it is an infield fly. Other than that, you can put a glove on a dog and until that dog gets under it and I think he can catch it with ordi-nary effort, it's not an infield fly. The person and his skill level makes absolutely zero, *zero*, difference."

However, he added that a big factor in invoking or not invoking the infield fly rule is the weather. "Sun is not a factor because once you get under it [a fly ball] and you're camped under it and I say you could catch it with ordinary effort, and now all of a sudden you happen to look into the sun, well, that's unfortunate. However, if you're camped under it but I know good and well we're in Wrigley and the wind is just howling that day, I'm watching how you're under it, but you're moving left and you're moving right, you're coming in, you're going back, even though it's just slightly, I'm taking that wind into consideration and you gotta remember this: it's not an infield fly until I say it's an infield fly. I don't have to call it the first second I think that it is; I can wait. If I think there are some things that are going on there, I can wait."

Umpires, in fact, are trained not to invoke this rule until the ball has reached its apex. Longtime ump Bruce Doane stated, "The reason we don't call an infield fly until it starts to come down is for that reason—to give yourself enough time to see that it's going to be ordinary effort by the infield or the outfielder."

The latest that an umpire can finally shout, "Infield fly is in effect," is after he has scrutinized all the factors he must consider, and according to Culbreth, that can be as late as "when it's actually in his glove. In theory I can wait until he's caught the ball because at any point up until then would've been [in some cases] crazy to call it.

"Remember this, too: the infield fly is not to protect the defense; it's to protect the offense. What you're trying to do is to make sure that they don't start letting balls purposely hit the ground and then doubling people off. At the same time, you're making the defensive guy do his job, but not having to do something that's ridiculously outrageous like trying to catch a baseball that's being blown all over the place."

Other factors come into play as well. Culbreth said that if, for instance, a pop up hits a bird in flight or if, say, "The ball's still going up and the third baseman and the shortstop run into each other and knock each other down, well, I don't know if they were camped under it or not, the ball was still going up, but I know this—a ball going up can do different things; a ball coming down can't do but one thing and that's continue to come down." As is the case with many rules, then, an umpire must take into consideration many factors.

(7) At first McCoy ruled the ball Randle blew on like a birthday candle foul, but the furious Royals manager, Jim Frey, argued the call and McCoy reversed himself. Randle's tactic is forbidden. Otis was awarded a single.

(8) Cubs catcher Randy Hundley thought the move by Selma was a balk, citing the rule that a pitcher is not permitted to throw to an unoccupied base. However, the crux of this issue is if Selma stepped off the rubber, which was the way the umps must have seen it, then he was permitted to make the throw. Unfortunately for the Cubs, the

169

throw had negative ramifications and a balk would have been less damaging to them.

Sal Giacomantonio, a veteran pro umpire, said, "Once the pitcher disengages from the rubber properly, he becomes an infielder and he can do pretty much whatever he wants, so that's legal.

"Now, there's also a rule that says that you cannot throw to an unoccupied base, but that is *from* the rubber. There is now an approved ruling that says you cannot throw to unoccupied base *unless* it's for the purposes of making a play on a runner.

"So let's say there are runners on first and second and the runner at second takes off a little bit earlier than what he normally would do and the pitcher notices this and as he's got his leg in air, before he commits to pitching at home, he could just step right to third and throw it—he's making a play on the runner from second. Now, there's some judgment in that because if the runner bluffs a run to third and the pitcher throws, then you could call a balk because there was no play there."

(9) Martin's running outside the lane definitely should have mattered, but it didn't. The rule states that a runner must be inside the lane when running to first base unless, of course, no play is being made on him—runners going for extra-base hits, for instance, don't need to worry about this rule. However, if a runner is not within the lane and he gets struck by a throw, he is ruled out and any other runner(s) must

return to his/their original base(s). On this particular play, though, home plate umpire Shag Crawford did not see (or believe there was a case of) Martin's interference, so the play stood and the Miracle Mets went up three games to one on Baltimore.

Craig Biggio feels the rule about the lane is foolish. "Why is that line [denoting the runners' lane] running down the side of the first base line in foul territory when the base is in fair? So you gotta run [in foul territory] and step in fair; that's pretty stupid."

In some amateur leagues, in order to avoid collisions around first base there are actually two bases—one is the bag normally used, but here is reserved for the defense to tag. The other one, which abuts the usual base, is set up in foul grounds and is only for the runners to step on as they ramble down the line.

(10) Yes, there is a penalty. Umpire Sal Giacomantonio pointed out Major League Baseball has been working on speeding up the pace of play "because the games are getting a little too long. So they actually instructed one of the umpires on the crew to keep track of how much time a pitcher spends in between pitches. If he takes too long, a ball is awarded to the batter."

Now, Papelbon did, in fact, get called for delaying games in 2009, violating the established guidelines regarding "pace-of-game." On one occasion in June he drew a $1,000 fine for taking too much time between being called into a game and throwing his first pitch—

a pitcher has, depending upon several circumstances dealing with televised games, between two minutes, five seconds and two minutes, thirty seconds to fire his initial pitch. He took a bit over three and a half minutes when he entered a game to start the ninth inning. Previously reprimanded and warned about his delays, he was also notified that if he violates the rule another time he will be fined $3,000, with a third infraction costing him $7,000 and a possible suspension.

Giacomantonio discussed yet another way a pitcher may be dealt with if he slows things down (or tries to do so). When a relief pitcher "gets summoned to come into the game by the umpire and he stays in the bullpen and takes an extra couple of pitches, then the umpires have the right to deduct [from] his eight warm-up pitches when he gets to the mound."

(11) There is no rule which prevents a fielder from kicking the ball. After all, normally what advantage would there be in doing that? The odds of a play like O'Neill's happening ever again are beyond astronomical.

(12) The run does not count. The automatic out, called when the runner left the base line, in effect counts exactly the same as if it had been made on a routine force play at second so the run will not stand.

(13) This is one of those calls you can't miss because the rule book states in such cases the ump is free to use his judgment in an effort to nullify the fan's interference. In other words, had the fan not touched the ball, what, in the umpire's opinion, would have unfolded? If he feels the runner would not have been able to tag and score from third, the umpire may freeze him there on the play. In our scenario the ball was hit so deeply Biggio would have scored so the umpire should allow the run to score. Of course, in such a situation, an unimpeded outfielder would no doubt opt to avoid making a catch in foul grounds which would cost his team the game—he could let it drop foul for a long, meaningless strike.

(14) Usually when a ball becomes lodged under a fence or, in this situation, disappears among vines, the correct call is a ground-rule double. In this instance, though, once Alou touched the ball, that ground rule is waived. The ball remained live and Everett took a round trip tour of the bases for an unusual inside-the-park home run. The scorer, recognizing Everett had earned two bases, ruled the play a double and a two-base error.

A ball can get lost in strange places along outfield walls. In a Prospect League contest a well-stroked ball took one hop in the outfield then hit the fence and made its way into a slit in a wind screen which covered the wall. The outfielder realized if he groped for the ball the batter would have probably had time to streak for at least three bases. So he calmly notified the umpire that the ball was out of play, conceding a ground-rule double to the opposition.

(15) The easy part of the call was Ferguson had earned a walk. It was also apparent that the ball was alive. Since Lacy had not left the field, he was entitled to score, but when Wynn had crossed the plate before Lacy, he had officially passed a runner. Bottom line: Wynn is out for his violation but Lacy's run stands.

(16) "I couldn't see it," Rash stated, "but I ruled it a fair ball, a home run. I said, 'I hope I'm making the right call.'" Rash, who got no argument on the play, was forced to rely on the location of the outfielder and common sense (remember, the outfielder was looking directly up from his position in fair territory) to make this tough call.

(17) No, stealing first base—actually, running the bases in a reverse order—is most certainly not legal. Believe it or not, though, this not only was once permitted, but it was pulled off several times. Probably the most famous, although not the first, instance came when Herman "Germany" Schaefer did this for the 1911 Washington Senators.

Schaefer, a big leaguer from 1901 to 1918, found he could get away with a base running ploy because there simply was no rule prohibiting it.

His most strange and famous antic took place back in the cobwebbed, early days of the game—sources vary, but August 4, 1911, is probably correct. After he reached first base in the ninth inning of a tie game that day, Washington had him on first and another man,

Clyde Milan, on third. The Senators put on the double steal which, they hoped, would allow the game-winning run to score. After all, this was the dead-ball era when a huge emphasis was placed on strategy and running, rather than on sheer slugging. So, Schaefer took off, but drew no throw from Chicago White Sox catcher Fred Payne.

It was then that the proverbial cartoon-like lightbulb began to burn brightly in Schaefer's brain. Why not run back to first base on the next pitch, he wondered. He was convinced such an odd, unexpected move would surely evoke a throw this time. Off he went, back to first on the very next pitch, and he made it, as if to refute the baseball cliché, "You can't steal first base." However, Milan remained stuck on third base and, of course, Schaeffer didn't really receive credit for a stolen base.

Undaunted, Schaefer lit off for second once more. Only this time, the story goes, the Sox defended the play well and retired Milan, who was trying to score. One source, though, has Schaefer getting caught in a rundown to draw attention away from Milan while yet another source says he did steal second, giving him a very unofficial three steals in the same inning.

Many years later the colorful Jimmy Piersall, who actually suffered from mental illness, hit his hundredth career home run on June 23, 1963, as a member of the New York Mets, then celebrated it by running the bases in their correct order but doing so while literally running them while facing backward.

18 Girardi argued that once Mora left the dirt circle, heading for his dugout, he had given up his right to race to first base on a dropped third strike case. He was correct and the inning came to a sudden halt.

19 From the clues given in this question, you may have guessed Ethier's run did count, scored before the third out of the inning occurred, but it could have been wiped off the scoreboard. If Arizona had appealed the play at third, pointing out that Ethier had never tagged up on the line drive, the umpires would have counted Ethier out for the fourth out of the inning and the upheld appeal would have negated his run.

However, once the Diamondbacks left the field, they lost their right to appeal and the run stood despite the fact Ethier had never tagged up—it was Arizona's responsibility to point that out to the umpires.

The exact ruling on when Arizona lost their right to appeal is this: the appeal has to take place before all of the infielders and the pitcher leave the field—they are considered to have done that once they all cross the foul lines. Even if just one infielder or the pitcher had remained on the field an appeal could have been made. Again, had they done that Pierre's third out would have been negated and the so-called "fourth out" on Ethier would have counted as having ended the inning, thus taking away his run scored.

Later, Lopez confessed that he didn't understand the rule when he tagged Pierre out rather than retire him by stepping on second base. The gift run allowed the Dodgers to tie the game at 1–1, and they went on to win 3–1.

20. Ennis would have been guilty of violating a rule if his glove had hit the ball perched on the fence. Contrary to what some fans believe, there is an infraction here *only* if the glove hits the ball—there is no penalty for merely throwing the glove at a baseball. The rule book specifies that if a fielder does strike a ball that has been hit by a batter and does so with a detached piece of equipment such as his glove, the batter is awarded three bases—Seminick had figured that three bases was better than giving Reese a home run. In the end, the Phils won the game and the NL flag before being swept by the dynastic Yankees.

While an argument could be made that the defense should not benefit from breaking a rule—after all, aside from scaling the wall à la Spiderman, there was no way to prevent an inside-the-park home run on this play—Seminick's idea, in theory, could have worked, holding Reese to three bases.

However, Fieldin Culbreth said it was very unlikely Ennis could have struck the ball with his glove and had it come back onto the field. He noted, too, that the top of the wall is, in his view, in play and not an automatic homer; it has not gone to the *other side* of the wall (or fence) for that to be the case. "To me, a ball that's a home run leaves the park, but if it hits the top of fence and bounces back in play [or stays perched there], it's in play. It's kind of up in no-man's-land, but it's still in play." In short, his call would be to deny Reese of an automatic home run.

He conceded that the concept of awarding a home run in this instance is a good example of is applying a little common sense to the rule book, but to go against the book here would result in nothing but grief.

The rule also stipulates three bases are awarded to the batter if a player touches a ball which had been hit in fair territory "with his cap, mask, or any part of his uniform detached from its proper place on his person. The ball is in play and the batter may advance to home plate at his peril."

So, if the fielder, say in a Little League contest, made a catch with his hat, it's three bases for the batter.

If a fielder intentionally touches a ball which was *thrown*, not hit, with the glove, cap, or detached article of his uniform, the penalty is two bases and, once more, the ball does remain in play. Finally, on a pitched ball the player is awarded one base.

(21) Maddon lost his designated hitter, meaning that his pitcher had to hit in that spot which happened to be the valuable number three slot in the batting order. So, Zobrist played third, Longoria sat the bench

(although after starting pitcher Andy Sonnanstine departed, he did enter the game at third base in the sixth inning), and Sonnanstine hit in what should have been Longoria's original spot.

Interestingly, Sonnanstine, who got the win, came through and helped himself with the bat—enjoying a 1-for-3 day. His hit was a long double to left, good for a run driven in during a five-run inning, helping the Rays win 7–5 at Tropicana Field.

The situation was so unusual Rick Roder, a former ump and current consultant to Major League Baseball, stated that the game's second base umpire who left the field to either call for help on the situation or to check on the rule book for clarification (a big reason the game was delayed thirteen minutes before the umpiring crew made a decision) was "looking for a rule that doesn't exist." In fact, *The Plain Dealer* reported in May 2009 that the game's circumstances "could lead to a change in the umpire's manual on how to handle the situation."

When Indians' manager Eric Wedge called the umpires' attention to Tampa Bay's violation, he may have made a tactical mistake—had he waited until Longoria, the intended designated hitter, stood in the box as the third hitter of the game, after Zobrist had already played in the field at third base (thus stripping his team of a DH) the ruling would have been different. That's because Longoria would have then been hitting in Sonnanstine's official spot in the order, making Longoria a pinch hitter for the pitcher. Therefore, the Rays would have had to replace their starter after just one inning. Further, the newspaper stated, "Some believe the umpires would have made Longoria ineligible," creating a further mess for Tampa Bay. As it was, Sonnanstine got to throw five and a third innings and Longoria did remain eligible to play.

Cleveland had considered waiting until Longoria batted, but they feared if he had come up with a key hit the umpiring crew would have permitted it to stand, because, technically, he was batting in his proper place in the lineup.

Then there was more. In an item labeled "Upon Further Review," *The Plain Dealer* of May 27 added this from Mike Port, vice president of big league umpiring—Longoria had, in fact, been incorrectly permitted to stay in the game. Port reached that conclusion after discussing it with umpire supervisors and allowed that "The umpires on the field that day had to decide at the moment. Not an easy assignment." The bottom line was this: Zobrist was fine, "already established at third base because they took the field in the top of the first." When Sonnanstine hit in the third slot in the order he was, in effect, replacing Longoria who should have been finished for the game. In short, it was a most befuddling situation.

As a side note, within a week Sonnanstine, an American League pitcher of all things, batted in three games. First was the time mentioned above. Then five days later he was the starting pitcher in an interleague game against the Marlins (and collected another hit), and his last day at the plate came the following day when he pinch hit against Florida, but whiffed with the bases loaded.

As yet another aside, the last time an American League starting pitcher was penciled into the batting order (aside from interleague play) was way back on September 23, 1976, when Ken Brett hit as a member of the White Sox. Brett, the older brother of George, was an excellent hitting pitcher, one employed to pinch hit even during the era of the designated hitter. A lifetime .262 hitter, he hit a home run in each of four consecutive starts for the Phillies in June 1973. As a matter of fact, in the game just prior to the first of those contests in which he homered, he hit a ground rule double as a pinch hitter, which an opposing outfielder later confessed was a home run. So he actually did hit a home run in five straight games in which he appeared, although he only got credit for five extra base hits over that span.

(22) This one is a much easier call than the previous situation. When Macha notified the umpires that Houston had batted out of order, the proper batter, Matsui, was declared out and Bourn was instructed to re-enter the batter's box to hit in his correct spot. On that at bat, Bourn drew a base on balls. So, in an unofficial way, Bourn reached base twice in a matter of moments. Meanwhile Matsui got charged with making an out without ever seeing a pitch that inning.

YOU'RE THE UMPIRE

(23) Some say the umpires reached a compromise, deciding to rule that a double play, not a triple play, had taken place. Both teams felt the umps got it wrong, and protested the game. The official word was this: The double play was recorded properly on Trillo at first, and then, amid the chaos, time out had been called. Although Howe tagged McBride, believing he had a triple killing, that out was not allowed because, by then, the ball was dead due to that time out. The inning, a very frustrating one for the Phillies, who felt shortchanged by the ruling, then ended when Larry Bowa grounded out. Eventually the Phils prevailed in ten frames, 5–3, to tie the series at two games apiece. They would win their next game, advance to the World Series, and win it all in six, knocking off the Kansas City Royals.

(24) Home plate umpire Jim Joyce let it be known that he believed that the momentum of DeRosa's swing took him across the plate and into the path of Oakland catcher Jason Kendall, thus interfering with the defense. According to the rules, not only is DeRosa retired on the strikeout, but the runner, Hairston, is automatically out, too. Thus the game ended on one pitch and an odd play with the A's the 7–6 victory.

(25) The ump working the Mota–Bench play was Harry Wendelsted, who immediately called catcher's interference on Bench as well as a balk on Gibbon. Mota's run scored and the game ended on a bizarre play.

182

Rule 7.07 states that when a runner off third base attempts to score on a steal or a squeeze play he shall be awarded home if the catcher (or, for that matter, any fielder) should step on, or in front of home plate while he is not in possession of the baseball—or, of course, if he makes contact with the batter or the bat. Officially the pitcher is charged with a balk, the batter gets first base, and the ball is dead.

Because the bases were loaded, Mota was forced to score, so his run naturally would count on either the balk call or the interference rule. Because Crawford was awarded a run driven in on the play, officially he scored on the interference, not the balk. Also, by rule, the batter is not charged with an at bat nor does he get credit for reaching base for the purposes of on-base percentage.

26 Because the tragic death of minor league third base coach Mike Coolbaugh in 2007—when he was struck in the head by a vicious line drive—prompted a rule change requiring coaches on the field to don a helmet, Montague certainly did have the right to insist on Bowa's wearing one. Bowa knew of the rule but didn't like it. His argument ended not only with him being ejected from the game, but also with Bowa being slapped with a suspension.

By the way, it's not all that unusual for the actions, ingenuity, or, in this case, the tragic misfortune of one man to lead to a rule change in baseball. An old tale has it that Pittsburgh Pirates third baseman Don Hoak once led off second base in the late 1950s or early 1960s, then took off on the next pitch. It was fouled off but Hoak, by then standing a step or two away from third base, refused to return to second. When an umpire asked him what he was doing, he reportedly said he was merely taking his lead off second for the next pitch. When the pitcher toed the rubber moments later, Hoak, so the story goes, hopped onto the bag at third, in effect stealing that base. At the time there was no rule to require a runner to back track to the base he held prior to the next pitch, but there is now.

Another famous case of a one-man rule change involved maverick St. Louis Browns owner Bill Veeck, but first a look at an old story about the last days of W. C. Fields, a man never known for being religious. A friend of his is said to have seen Fields leafing through a Bible. Knowing Fields was on his deathbed, the friend gently asked if he had finally found religion. The comedian scowled then drawled, "No, I'm merely looking for loopholes." Well, Veeck scoured the rule book with the same intense scrutiny of Fields.

Veeck, famous for his "I try not to break the rules but merely to test their elasticity" quote, once signed Eddie Gaedel, a three-foot, seven inch, sixty-seven-pound theatrical midget, to a big league contract. Of course it was a promotional gag of the inventive, controversial Veeck, but Gaedel *was* permitted to bat. Wearing the jersey number "1/8," he drew a walk on four pitches (just as Veeck had, of course, envisioned), was replaced by a pinch runner and, due to a new rule which was quickly drawn up, would never again appear in a game.

The rule could be labeled "No Midgets Allowed" as it prohibited such antics as Veeck pulled. Of course signing and using a very short player is fine if he's a legitimate ballplayer. Fred Patek, for example, was listed at a perhaps-generous 5 feet 4 inches, but was a solid player and was, of course, allowed to play pro ball.

(27) The run does count. Some fans get this play mixed up, thinking Fielder's third out was a force play, but it isn't—he wasn't *forced* to go to second on the fly ball nor was he forced to return to first, by the definition of the word "force." Sure, he *had* to get back to first before the ball beat him or he was out, but, again, he was not forced. Ergo, count the run, end the inning on the double play.

(28) First of all, on a hidden-ball play the reason the trick is doomed if anyone calls time out is simple—the play can't work because the ball, naturally, would not be in play during a time out, nor would it be again until the pitcher toed the rubber to resume action and, at that point, he'd have to have the (now unhidden) ball in his possession in order for the game to restart.

Secondly, even if a time out isn't called, in order for this act of leg-erdemain to be run legally a rule states that a pitcher cannot deceive the runner(s). The pitcher may try to dupe the runner by being on the mound without the baseball, but he may not take a position, said collegiate ump Doug Nauer, "on or astride the rubber." Now, in college ball, by NCAA rules, he can't even be "on the dirt circle without the ball." If a pitcher violates the rule, this trick play, even if run successfully, will be voided and the umpire's call is an emphatic, "Balk!"

In short, a college pitcher, in order to carry out the chicanery called for on this play, must stay off the hill—stall, confer with a teammate, stomp around the infield grass as if upset with himself or the previous play, or do *anything* else in his acting repertoire but go on the mound, while the big leaguer can pull off similar histrionics as long as he doesn't get on or straddle, the rubber.

In 1998, Williams, then with the Diamondbacks, actually had another runner fooled on this same play, but Arizona pitcher Felix Rodriguez botched it by going to the rubber prematurely and Colorado's Neifi Perez, instead of suffering the ignominy of being duped, scored on the balk.

Cleveland coach Johnny Goryl was very impressed by Williams when he conned Hansen, "He did a helluva job with it. That was the first time I saw it done in the big leagues in a *long* time."

Cleveland's Travis Fryman later stated quite simply that such a trick can work because "most players aren't good base runners." He said that if a runner is alert and doesn't stray off a base when the pitcher isn't on the mound, he simply can't get suckered by the hidden ball play.

(29) Yes, the ball is alive, so Gibson was advancing at his own risk. Here, the equipment is, in effect, part of the playing field. The out sticks.

(30) It is a legal catch, but because he left the playing field, any runners on base would be given an extra base on the play.

(31) Because there were already two men retired in the inning, the third strike officially closes out the inning and the run would not score. Had there been fewer than two outs, the ball would be dead, the batter would be out on strikes, but the runner scores on the brazen steal of home.

Two items for trivia lovers: 1) Maury Wills had the unusual middle name of Morning; 2) Juan Marichal never finished higher than eighth in Cy Young Award voting and that was in 1971, long after he accomplished seasons such as this: 25–8 (1963); 21–8 (1964); 22–13 (1965); 25–6 (1966); and 26–9 (1968). In fact, over his entire career he garnered one vote for the Cy Young—*one*. Imagine winning just over 80 percent of your decisions one year (1966) to lead your league; firing a league-leading ten shutouts one season (1965); and topping the league with a minuscule 2.10 ERA another year (1969), and *never* getting a single vote for the prestigious pitching trophy over those marvelous seasons. Unbelievable.

32 The play, as described, stands. There is a rule which prevents a fielder such as Counsell from *purposely* dropping a ball, then making, say, a double play, but that doesn't apply here where it is the responsibility of the batter to hustle as soon as he popped the ball up to avoid a ploy by the defense to get a cheap double play.

Umpire Sal Giacomantonio elaborated on the rule about purposely dropping a ball in the air. "Anytime there's a force situation where runners have to move up, even first and third, you're not going to allow the defense to do an intentional dropped ball, but they can let it drop to the ground—they can't just catch it to knock it down and drop it." If a defender, for example, let a ball hit in his mitt then dropped it intentionally, "you'd rule the batter out and put the runners back."

He added that on a bunt a defensive player may "let it hit the ground, that's not an intentionally dropped ball." Some shrewd pitchers, for example, deke the offense, acting as if they're about to catch the popped up bunt only to let it fall to the grass before firing the ball to get the lead runner and perhaps even start a double play if the man who bunted the ball, believing the bunt was about to be caught, doesn't hustle.

33 The umpire that day decreed Lundblade to be safe. There was, after all, no way he was going to punish the team on offense by allowing the tag at the plate to be ruled an out.

OBSCURE RULES AND SITUATIONS

Giacomantonio speculated that the umpire who made that call (because, again, there is certainly no rule that covers such a bizarre play), may have invoked "the old 9.01c rule, which means anything that's not currently ruled on, that's not covered in the rule books, the umpires have the authority to make a ruling on it. Obviously, in a situation like that—I mean, what the hell, a potato in the hand! That's just ridiculous."

Bresnahan's creative ways were certainly not appreciated; he truly had made a travesty of the game. As a result, he was kicked out of the game for his unsportsmanlike act, fined $50 by his manager, Orlando Gomez, and he was soon released from the Williamsport squad.

Giacomantonio found it difficult to believe such a play took place at such a high level of baseball. "It's embarrassing for the program—people would think that the coaches are instructing that."

Culbreth noted that he had never been a part of an umpiring crew that had to invoke the "travesty of the game" rule. Bruce Froemming added, "My umpiring was too serious to talk about that. I never had a situation where I had a travesty. I had situations where guys got out of control with language and whatever, but I had enough pride and enough credibility throughout my career the way I ran my game that I didn't see any of that."

However, the travesty rule does come into play on occasion. Veteran umpire Bruce Doane recalled using the rule against "one of the better [semi-pro] teams in the country. Their manager was getting guys picked off on purpose because they were so far ahead and he just wanted to end the inning so they could shorten the game and get the heck out of there, finish the game and move on. So he'd have guys just stand there and get picked off. I didn't particularly care for that so I squashed that. I said, 'The next time you do something like that I'm going to run you, then we won't have to worry about that kind of stuff. We're not going to make a circus out of this.' As far as a travesty of the game, that was the only time I've ever addressed it with a manager."

Getting back to Bresnahan, just two nights later his seventh-place team ran a promotion during its final game of the year. Any fan that brought a potato to the park was admitted to the game for one dollar. Bresnahan even made an appearance, autographing potatoes with the inscription, "This spud's for you."

His fame, or infamy, quickly spread and he was appeared on David Letterman's show and on an NBC pre-game show.

In 1988 he again visited the site of his potato–throwing incident, Bowman Field, where, this time he was honored, not vilified, by the team. They painted his uniform number of the outfield fence. A team spokesperson quipped, "He's probably the only .149 hitter to ever have his jersey retired."

(34) What the umpire, Dale Scott, couldn't miss here was the ball went into the stands, but only because a fan made it do so. The ump ruled fan

interference and allowed Hannahan to score from first base because, as acting manager Jeff Datz elucidated, "[Scott] told me that, in his opinion, Johnson's ball would have gotten into the right-field corner without the interference. That would have allowed Hannahan to score."

(35) The correct call is umpire's interference. It is a play so rare a veteran ump such as Fieldin Culbreth said he has never called it in the majors while working the field and only "on myself behind home plate about two, maybe three times, and that was just the old [situation of] the catcher rears back to throw it, hits you, and that impedes his throw—that's interference and the guy has to go back unless the catcher puts him out."

So, in our situation, O'Nora immediately, and quite correctly, called interference on himself (making the ball dead), sent Victorino back to first, and, because the pitch, which does count, had been low and inside, announced that the count on Utley was now 2–0.

Now, let's say a catcher saw that a base runner had a fantastic jump on a steal—could he, realizing he'd have no chance to gun him out, purposely initiate umpire's interference to thwart the stolen base? Professional umpire Sal Giacomantonio said, "They could do that, but actually you [sometimes] see a catcher try to initiate contact with a batter to [cause an umpire] to call batter's interference on the throw to second."

YOU'RE THE UMPIRE

Usually there's enough room separating the catcher from the umpire, which prevents a catcher from trying the previously mentioned tactic, but "if the umpire feels that the catcher intentionally did [make contact with him], he does not have to award umpire's interference on that, but I've never heard of a catcher trying to draw umpire's interference."

Fieldin Culbreth took it one step further, saying he doesn't know how an umpire could ascertain whether the catcher initiated contact with an ump. He added, though, "If I thought he did it on purpose, and I guarantee you this—I would have to know without fail that he did that [before ignoring the call of umpire's interference]."

As for a crafty catcher getting away with initiating batter's interference, it can happen, but umpires are, said Giacomantonio, "trained to observe what's going on at the plate and what happens is a batter's momentum—say he swings and misses an outside pitch—will take him a little bit across the plate. If the catcher is smart enough, he's going to step up and throw and kind of make sure he draws some contact [with the batter]. If a catcher really goes out of his way to draw it, then we just give the 'safe' signal and say, 'That's nothing.'" In other words, the play continues because "the defense initiated the contact, the batter was where he was supposed to be, he didn't do anything to effect the catcher, and the catcher did it to himself. You're going to let the play stand."

(36) "We always say you don't want an even number of calls at one base—meaning you don't want two calls at any one base," Giacomantonio noted with a chuckle. "It rarely happens, but when it does the ruling is the umpire in chief has the final say after getting input from all of other umpires, so it's not like automatically one person's call; it's more that the two get together and they figure out whose call it should have been and who was in the best position to see the call." The key is getting it right and "trying to make the best of a bad situation."

Ryan Burich has umpired amateur games for nearly fifteen years now and recalled a time he worked a championship series in the Northwoods League as part of a six-man crew and ran into the same situation Bragan mentioned. "I was on third base for Game One and there was a shot down the left field line, past the bag, a definite fair or foul decision. I'm right in position and I point fair, and when I'm watching the ball, I turn around and see the left field umpire pointing foul."

Burich explained the outcome of this play, "Since I pointed fair right away, and I was the first one to call a fair ball, the ball was in fair play—I was right on top of the play, it was my call, but the coach came out—he never really yelled at me—but he yelled at the guy who was down the left field line. You get that a lot, especially at the lower levels where umpires are new." Giacomantonio said that in this case there would be a third man, the home plate ump, who could be called into the discussion. If he said he felt it was, for example, a fair ball, "now you're going to have two guys that thought it was fair and one that thought it was foul and then they need to decide how to fix that.

"The unfortunate thing is it's a lot easier to make a fair ball foul, but it's very difficult to make a foul ball fair because then where are you going to put the runner(s)? [Reconstructing where runners should be] becomes a guessing game." In other words, if a ball was initially called fair and play continued before the umpires decided to rule the questionable hit foul, they simply send any runners and the batter back, but if they call it foul right away, then realize it was actually a fair ball, the crew would then have the mess on their hands of where to place the runners.

As Giacomantonio added, "It's a delicate situation. If you're going to make a mistake, it's obviously a little bit easier if you just leave the ball in play and see where everything pans out. Then if the call needs to be changed to a foul, you just put the batter back to bat and add a strike on him."

Another umpire, Doug Nauer, commented "very seldom do two umpires have opposite calls. Having a good pre-game meeting and [with] umpires knowing their responsibilities would cut down on the chances of multiple calls happening on one play. The umpire in chief basically has the last say so, but the main thing is to get the right call.

"Say on a NCAA two- or three-man umpiring crew there's a man on first base and there's a base hit to center field and the center fielder is making a play on the runner going from first to third. That's the home plate umpire's call to make. Say the umpire at home plate missed his rotation and he was supposed to be at third and the guy from second notices, so he starts to move toward third just to help make a call there. All of a sudden the guy at home plate starts to come up then [to third] and they both make a call. In a situation like that, that was the home plate umpire's responsibility; he was supposed to be there [at third]. So it would be his call, but if the second base umpire was trying to cover for him they'd probably have to confer."

Nauer added that some calls, no matter who makes them, must stand. "Once a ball is called foul, it's a foul ball except for home runs. You can't overrule a foul ball and make it a fair ball—a home run ball [however] can be overturned."

He summarized, "Communication is the key thing and as officials get more and more experience, and especially at the professional level, you are most likely not going to see two different calls on the same play." Fluke plays are bound to happen, but not too often especially considering the myriad plays that take place each day.

Also, sometimes two umpires will glance at each other and one will decide to take charge and make the call, avoiding two men making different calls on a play. "Just get it right," concluded Nauer. "That's what the bottom line is on that."

(37) No, there are established standards for the wearing of protective elbow pads. For example, the size of the pad when it is measured lying flat must not exceed ten inches in length. The most important regulation is this: "No player may wear a non-standard elbow protection pad, or any pad designed to protect the upper or lower arm, unless the player has an existing elbow or other arm injury and the Club has obtained the approval of the Commissioner's Office to wear that particular non-standard equipment."

In addition, a physician has to provide a report with a diagnosis of the injury and his estimate of how long the player in question needs to wear the pad. Finally, if a team feels an opponent has a player who has donned a protective elbow pad which in any way violates the rules, they must notify the home plate umpire. Such action triggers an investigation and, if there is a violation of the rules, the team "will be subject to discipline."

(38) Once the ball is dropped with a runner or runners on base, it's a balk. Had nobody been on base the rule is this: if the ball fell and rolled across a foul line, it counts as a pitch, an automatic ball, but if it doesn't cross either foul line, it's a no pitch.

(39) Once the pitcher who is on the rubber, working out of the stretch position with a man or men on base, begins his motion prior to making a pitch or before making a throw to a base, he must, in his

natural delivery, complete his action or it's a balk. Had he not begun his motion to throw the ball—if he was, say, simply peering in to get the sign—he could step off the rubber to stop play, but once he removes his bare hand from its position inside the glove as described, he must make his throw, he can't simply stop.

With no one on base it's a different story as you will sometimes see a pitcher start his windup and, for example, not feel right about his mechanics, and stop in mid stream—that's fine. After all, a pitcher can't balk with nobody on.

(40) No matter how the contact was made, a defender may not touch, be touched by the runner as described, or impede a base runner caught in a run down unless, of course, he is in the act of tagging him. Furcal did not have the ball so he should have moved a bit out of the way—he can't block the base path here. Therefore, Pierzynski should be given second base (but see the answer to the next question for more details).

(41) It doesn't matter if Pierzynski was advancing to the next base or retreating to the one he had just come from—once he and the defender make contact (as described in questions 40 and 41), he is awarded the next base, never the one he had just left.

Note, though, that there is some judgment involved in such matters on the part of the umpires. Fieldin Culbreth elaborated, "If there's a run down between bases and a player gets in the way of a runner, that's obstruction. However, there's a provision that if the runner goes out of his way to make that contact, to assure that contact happens, then he's out. You're not going to reward him by calling obstruction and giving him the base beyond the one legally touched."

(42) No. The two runners are fine, but Francoeur had no right to run the bases. The only time a batter may try to reach first (or beyond) when a third strike isn't directly fielded by the catcher is when there are two men out or when there are fewer than two gone and first base is unoccupied at the time of the pitch. Francoeur is out, erase him from the bases.

Of course, in reality, Molina is much too smart to make such a blunder, but if he had, it would have cost his team dearly and saddled him with a throwing error.

In a related play, the Cardinals were playing the Dodgers on August 17, 2009, and sent Colby Rasmus to pinch run for Matt Holliday at first. Rick Ankiel was at the plate facing Jonathan Broxton with one man out. Broxton fanned Ankiel with Rasmus running on the play and, when catcher Russell Martin's throw deflected off the glove of shortstop Rafael Furcal into right field, Rasmus ended up at third. Now an uninformed fan might argue that, with Rasmus running prior to Broxton's release of the baseball, first base was unoccupied by the time Ankiel whiffed, so he was entitled to run to that bag if the catcher did not come up with the third strike cleanly. However, the rule considers the placement of the runner at the start of the play—first base was clearly occupied and, again, with fewer than two outs, a batter cannot attempt to reach that base after striking out in that situation.

(43) The call here, and it was a correct one, was to award two bases to the runners, forcing Zobrist to trot back to third base even though he could have made it home with ease—as Rays manager Joe Maddon later stated, "I could've scored from the dugout on that play." Zobrist was soon stranded, but Evan Longoria blasted a walk off home run in the thirteenth inning to make the matter moot.

The rule book indicates that when a ball is thrown into the seating area "or into a bench (whether or not the ball rebounds into the field), or over or under or through a fence . . ." or, in this situation, into the bag, the ball is dead and the runner(s) gets to advance two bases. The umpires are to award the bases from the position of the runner(s) when the ball was pitched in every case where the wild throw was the first play made by an infielder—the runners' position at the time of the ball becoming dead is immaterial.

Maddon declared that from that play forward equipment would be stored better, where it could not interfere with play. "It's a one-in-a-million situation," he began, "but you can lose pennants by one game."

YOU'RE THE UMPIRE

The announcers that day initially vilified the umpires for botching the play, but they, unlike the umps, just didn't know the rules. Major league umpire Fieldin Culbreth, graciously pointed out, "I don't think that any announcer rips us because of any other reason than they just don't understand the rules themselves, but they're certain that they do; they're not out to just make me look bad. I don't think that when they open their mouth they go, 'We're just going to rip this guy.' I don't think they would sit there and say what they're saying if they just knew how wrong they were because nobody likes being wrong, but the truth is until I went to umpire school, I had no idea how little of the rules that I did know. I mean, it's one thing to give, say, the definition of obstruction, yet it's another to go out there, see it, apply it, and then tell you what it is. I can tell you that obstruction is this, this, and this. Well, that's the easy part. However, when you go out there and you have to see what's impeding, what got this way, and how it got this way, now you're talking about a horse of a different color. The guys on TV are no different than I was at the time I was when I first got into the game—you think you know everything in the world about baseball because some of them played it, some of them didn't, but the truth is they know very, very, very little about the complex rules."

He said announcers know the basics, and could easily recognize that "if a guy's trying to catch the baseball, if a runner runs over him that's not allowed," but when other factors come into play such as what to do with other runners on base when the fielder is bowled over, "that's where they get confused."

Instead of assuming the umpires are incorrect, said Culbreth, announcers should realize that "the umpires will straighten it out. The thing is when an announcer says what he does on TV, that's what the millions of people that are watching believe. I don't get a chance to come back five minutes later and say, 'By the way, this announcer was wrong.' So I'm down there ruling absolutely correctly and this guy's up there saying, 'I don't know why they're doing that,' and what do you think the public believes?"

(44) In this situation, the runner is awarded one base as punishment for the defense having used a piece of equipment to touch (and aid themselves in securing) the pitched ball.

Giacomantonio once saw this same play involving a lackadaisical major league catcher using his mask to retrieve a ball which had trickled a short distance from him after first looking up to make sure a runner off first was not trying to advance. "The umpire, Jeff Nelson, awarded the runner second base because the catcher used detached equipment to help him field the ball."

Marty Dunn, a coach for the Chillicothe (Ohio) Paints of the Prospect League, recalled another similar infraction, though not on a pitched ball. "There was a play with the ball coming to the plate and the catcher used his mask to stop the ball." Again, a player simply may not make such a move.

(45) "You're not going to let the defense benefit from that," Giacomantonio said. "You'll put the runner back at the base where he was leading off from and you'll probably throw out the guy who threw that ball [onto the field]."

(46) "Once you have interference," stated Doane, "the ball's dead. We sent the runner back to third base, called the hitter out, and you're not supposed to advance on any interference, pretty much, but the runner that went from first to second base had already stolen second and had gone to third on the throw to the plate. We brought him back to second." He ruled that the interference had "happened *after* he was down to second base."

(47) Doane explained what he did that day: "I just told both managers, 'You're going to have to work with me on this,' so I let the runner score from third because he would've scored anyhow on the balk, and actually I let them get the guy out on the rundown. Right, wrong, or otherwise, I didn't have much recourse. I guess I could have lied and said I got a balk, just made up a balk, but I didn't do it that way."

Doane elaborated that it wasn't a balk because the pitcher threw to first base. Doane had simply pulled the trigger too swiftly in calling it a balk. "He just did it so quick I was just jumping out of my shoes because at that time we were emphasizing that particular rule." Doane was honest enough to admit that, like all humans, umpires do make mistakes occasionally and he did straighten things out.

(48) Cox is doomed to get thumbed once again in this situation. Long ago, arguments over balls and strikes became so frequent and time consuming, baseball decided to make on-the-field discussions/arguments over pitch calling grounds for automatic ejection.

Managers (and others) can still bellow out protests, within reason, from the bench, but still risk being kicked out if they persist too long or if, for example, their behavior and/or language ignites an umpire's fuse. Many umpires simply ignore most complaints while others, those said to have "rabbit ears," are more sensitive to and upset by criticism.

The truth is while most umps are quite tolerant of some grumbling, they are understanding only up to a point—usually they'll issue a warning to a specific complainant or sometimes to the bench in general, but they don't have to do this before running someone from a game.

(49) Carroll said that on the play the runner was ruled safe. "The guy was trying to go around [the tag] and [in doing so] he completely missed the base." So, the Indians took the ball and stepped on first while the runner was still beyond the bag, but "he was considered safe,"

concluded Carroll, "because once he goes past the bag, regardless of not touching it, you have to tag him."

Sal Giacomantonio went into a bit more depth. "Once the batter-runner passes a base, he is considered to have touched it regardless if he actually makes contact with it or not. The play now turns into an appeal play where the defense has to verbally announce to the umpire and tag (with possession of the ball) either the runner or the base that was missed.

"The umpire would initially rule the runner safe because he was never put out [tagged]. At this point, the defense has to appeal that the runner missed first base."

The easiest thing the first baseman could have done would have been to track down the runner as he came back from overrunning the base and tag him as a way to appeal that he had never touched first base, but the first baseman cannot simply touch first base. For that matter, to get the out here the first baseman could also have touched the bag *and* declared he was making an appeal.

Giacomantonio continued that in such plays the umpire is supposed to rule safe initially "until the defense actually appeals the play which is kind of strange, isn't it?" The logic seems to be that because the defense did not retire him, then he's not out. If he's not out, then he must be considered safe—at least for the moment.

"Plays at home are treated differently. If the guy misses the plate and the catcher misses the tag, we're instructed to make no call." The ump won't make a call until the runner goes back and touches the plate, the defense makes a play and retires the runner, or if neither the offense nor the defense takes action, the run would count once the next pitch took place.

(50) Umpire Bill Jackowski, who was working the bases that day, made the ruling: "Stan the Man" was out because he had been tagged by Banks using the original ball—the one that was in play from the start of this unique play.

In a 2009 interview, Solly Hemus, who was managing the Cardinals that day, said he protested the game due to what he labeled was "just a freak play [hinging on] a decision the umpire made which I thought was wrong, but is neither here nor there now." He was correct that the call was inconsequential in that the Cards eventually won by a 4-1 score, making his protest moot.

ADRIAN GONZALEZ

ACKNOWLEDGMENTS

I'd like to give a special thanks to all the umpires from various levels of baseball who lent their time and expertise to my project. They include major league umpires Fieldin Culbreth, who gets a big nod of appreciation for the extensive, detailed help he gave me, and Bruce Froemming. Thanks also go out to minor league umpires Homer Rash, Tyler Bolick, Ed Rogers; Sal Giacomantonio and Bruce Doane of the Frontier League; collegiate umpire Doug Nauer; as well as to Ohio umpires Pete Carbonaro, Brett Locher, and Ryan Burich. Thanks also to Andy Jarvis, manager of the North Coast Knights and Brian Mannino and Marty Dunn of the Chillicothe Paints, all three of the Prospect League. Other people interviewed who were helpful include Hank Aaron, John Kuenster, Stu Miller, Solly Hemus, Bobby Bragan, Jesse Orosco, Craig Biggio, Alex Grammas, Steve Foucault, Wayne Krenchicki, and Cameron Castro. A tip of the cap to my friend Al Shaffer for his help setting up several interviews and to Jamie Santo for his astute copyedit. Finally, a thank you also goes out to my editor, Mark Weinstein, for his help on this, our sixth project together.

ABOUT THE AUTHOR

Wayne Stewart was born and raised in Donora, Pennsylvania, a town that has produced a handful of big league baseball players, including Stan Musial and the father-son Griffeys. As a matter of fact, Stewart was on the same Donora High School baseball team as Ken Griffey Sr. as a good glove, no stick bench player. Stewart now lives in Lorain, Ohio, with his wife Nancy. They have two sons, Sean and Scott, and one grandchild, Nathan.

Stewart has covered the sports world since 1978, and has written twenty-five books to date and over 500 articles for publications such as *Baseball Digest, USA Today/Baseball Weekly, Boys' Life,* and Beckett Publications. Furthermore, Stewart has appeared, as a baseball expert and historian, on Cleveland's Fox 8 and on an ESPN Classic television show on Bob Feller.

SOURCES

Books and Booklets:

As They See 'Em by Bruce Weber

Babe Ruth: A Biography by Wayne Stewart

Baseball Bafflers by Wayne Stewart

Baseball Oddities by Wayne Stewart

Baseball Puzzlers by Wayne Stewart

The Best of Baseball Digest by John Kuenster

Big League Baseball Puzzlers by Dom Forker

Great Hitting Pitchers compiled by the Society for American Baseball Research

Green Cathedrals by Philip J. Lowry

Indians on the Game by Wayne Stewart

Match Wits with Baseball Experts by Wayne Stewart

Pitching Secrets of the Pros by Wayne Stewart

Tales from the Dodgers Dugout by Carl Erskine

Umpires by John C. Skipper

Working at the Ballpark by Tom Jones

Wrigleyville by Peter Golenbock

YOU'RE THE UMPIRE

Magazines:
Baseball Digest
Sporting News
USA Today Sports Weekly

Newspapers:
The Atlanta Journal and Constitution
The Chronicle-Telegram, Elyria, Ohio
The Plain Dealer, Cleveland
Rocky Mountain News, Denver

Web sites:
baseball-almanac.com
baseballhalloffame.org
baseball-reference.com
baseballanalysts.com
boston.com
espngo.com
mlb.com
pressbox.mlb.com
retrosheet.org
time.com
wikipedia.com